Languages of the Pre-Columbian Antilles

Languages of the Pre-Columbian Antilles

JULIAN GRANBERRY
GARY S. VESCELIUS

THE UNIVERSITY OF ALABAMA PRESS
Tuscaloosa

Typeface: Minion

∞

The paper on which this book is printed meets the minimum requirements of American National Standard for Information Science–Permanence of Paper for Printed Library Materials, ANSI Z39.48–1984.

Library of Congress Cataloging-in-Publication Data

Granberry, Julian.
    Languages of the Pre-Columbian Antilles / Julian Granberry, Gary S. Vescelius.
        p. cm.
    Includes bibliographical references and index.
    ISBN 0-8173-1416-4 (cloth : alk. paper) — ISBN 0-8173-5123-X (pbk. : alk. paper)
1. Indians of the West Indies—Antilles, Greater—Languages. 2. Taino language—Antilles, Greater. I. Vescelius, Gary S. II. Title.
    PM5099.A68G73 2004
    409′.729—dc22

                                                                                    2004002838

Contents

Figures

Tables

Preface

The chapters in this volume, originally written as separate essays at different times over a period of years, have been re-edited together to suggest the formulation of a testable language-based hypothesis concerning the origins of the Pre-Columbian cultures and peoples of the Caribbean Antilles. Unlike *Languages of the West Indies,* written in 1977 by the dean of Antillean language studies, the late Douglas Taylor, or the perceptive articles by contemporary researchers such as Arnold Highfield of the University of the Virgin Islands (Highfield 1993, 1995, 1997), which concentrate largely on matters linguistic per se, the present volume is oriented toward the analysis of language forms not for their own sake but, instead, as a pragmatic tool toward elucidation of the physical, ethnic, and linguistic origins of their users.

Rather than include the islands of the entire Caribbean region, only the Antilles have been considered in the present study: Cuba, Jamaica, Hispaniola, and Puerto Rico (the Greater Antilles); the Commonwealth of the Bahamas and the Crown Colony of the Turks and Caicos (the Greater Antillean outliers of the Lucayan Islands) and the Cayman Islands; the Virgin Islands and the Leeward and Windward Islands (the Lesser Antilles); and Barbados, and Trinidad and Tobago. The peoples and languages of the southern Caribbean islands (Los Testigos, Isla Blanquilla, Margarita, Cubagua, Coché, La Tortuga, Islas los Roques, Aruba, Bonaire, and Curaçao) and the western Caribbean islands (Cancún, Cozumel, the Bay Islands, Islas del Maíz, San Andrés, and Providencia) have not been included primarily because they did not play a major role in the settlement of the Antilles proper, that stepping-stone chain of islands that leads from the northeastern littoral of South America and Trinidad northward and westward through the Caribbean Sea toward the Florida and Yucatán Peninsulas. Those southern and western Caribbean islands were, of course, important in their own right in pre-Columbian times, but their peoples and languages derived from sources largely different from those of the Antilles proper and their energies directed more toward their adjacent mainlands than to the vast arc of islands to their north and east.

More attention has also been devoted to the peoples of the Greater Antilles, the Taíno and their predecessors, than to the Eyeri of the Lesser Antilles simply because Eyeri origins, both archaeologically and linguistically, are considerably clearer and more straightforward than the linguistic and archaeological origins of the Greater Antillean peoples. This is not, of course, to imply that the archaeological picture of cultural developments in the Lesser Antilles is one of crystal clarity, for it certainly is not, but at least the problem of ethnolinguistic origins is relatively uncomplicated (see Allaire 1977, 1990, 1991; Rouse and Allaire 1979; Taylor and Hoff 1980).

The emergent hypothesis concerning the aboriginal settlement of the Antilles, outlined in Chapter 5 for the Greater Antilles and summarized in Chapter 11 for the entire Antillean region, is based on both archaeological and linguistic evidence. No new archaeological information is introduced, but the bulk of the language evidence, particularly for the Greater Antilles, while available for nearly 500 years, has been neither fully nor critically examined. The latter evidence is, therefore, the primary focus of the discussion. The conclusions presented, it should be constantly kept in mind, are decidedly not a statement of formal theory but simply the correlation of a body of data not looked at before as a unit, data that are in need of considerable further investigation and examination to help elucidate Antillean cultural origins.

It is unquestionably the case that the conclusions reached in this volume, and perhaps some of our methods of data-treatment, may not be endorsed by all archaeologists and linguists. This, we hope, is not because of any mishandling of the data or peculiar theoretical and methodological biases on our part, but, rather, because some of the language data dealt with are so extremely scanty and the language–culture relationships proposed are so very distant in time. We are well aware of this, yet the data are there and should be handled in some manner. The interplay of language and the rest of culture is part of the unsolved warp of the Antillean past, and rather than simply leave it at that, as has generally been the case in the past, it seems justifiable and desirable to look at it with the premises and methods of modern archaeological and linguistic analysis. Testing of the hypothesis would, beyond doubt, help toward an ultimate reliable definition of population movements in the pre-Columbian Antilles, something we do not have at present.

The first and primary assumption made (one not palatable to some trained solely in archaeology nor to practitioners of the many nontraditional, non-empirical brands of linguistics so popular nowadays) is that language plays a delimiting (but not determining) role with regard to culture content, including a society's choice of artifactual inventory and its typological and stylistic expression. Language provides a kind of cultural filter which seems to set boundaries outside of which its speakers are unable to go, perhaps unable even to imagine, without, at the same time, constraining or dictating the specific social-cultural choices that members of the group may make within the bounds of its language/cultural filter.

Such a premise is well borne out by substantive research spanning the period from at least the 1940s through the 1980s by the sociologist Bengt Danielsson (1949); the physical anthropologist W. W. Howells (1966); the physical anthropologists H. Gershowitz, J. V. Neel, F. M. Salzano, and Richard S. Spielman, together with the well-known South American linguist Ernest C. Migliazza (Spielman, Migliazza and Neel 1974; Salzano, Neel, Gershowitz and Migliazza 1977); the ethnologist Ernest Burch (1975); and the archaeologists Betty J. Meggers and Clifford Evans (1980) among others. That research repeatedly indicates that within any well-defined geographical area the expectation and norm is that people speaking the same or closely related languages tend to intermarry, that is, to participate in a common, highly specific gene pool, and consequently, as well, to show similar socioeconomic and related nonmaterial culture traits and common artifactual preferences. Conversely, archaeologically defined artifactual inventories within such well-defined sociogeographical areas are most likely to have been created and developed, including the adaptation of diffused traits, by speakers of the same or closely related languages. It is, regardless of the details of the phenomenon, the exception which needs explanation.

Because of the above points, not only have copious quotes from the referenced Spanish documentary sources been included, but the original Spanish texts have also been used, so that the basis of the assumptions (and also the translations) may be checked. This is a courtesy due the reader when such a small database is involved, with apologies for the length this sometimes entails.

The statements in the chapters of this book are the result of both individual and joint research. Both authors began their work in the years between 1947 and 1951, when they were classmates in the Department of Anthropology at Yale University under Irving Rouse and Wendell Bennett in archaeology; George Murdock, Ralph Linton, Raymond Kennedy, Clellan Ford, and, from time to time, Margaret Mead in ethnology; and Leonard Bloomfield, Bernard Bloch, Julian Obermann, Albrecht Goetze, and, later, Floyd Lounsbury in linguistics. In Granberry's case, Antillean work has continued from that date to the present; in the case of Vescelius, from then until his untimely death in 1982. The statements are particularly the result of joint research by the authors during the 1970s.

While the individual chapters as they appear here were written by Granberry after Vescelius's death, they were prepared from outlines, copious notes, and partly formulated or completed essays written separately or jointly by Vescelius and Granberry over a period of many years, bringing together the considered, data-based, consensus archaeological, and linguistic analysis and opinions of both authors.

The senior author would like to thank many individuals who have over the years listened to earlier versions of the materials presented in this volume, volunteered helpful data and information, and offered various kinds of criticism. Most important is Linda Sickler Robinson, without whom Vescelius's valuable notes might have vanished into oblivion. Her friendship and kindness have been most appreciated. Paul and Joan Albury, Sandy Alexiu, Peter Barratt, Mary Jane Berman, Ellen Bethell, Ripley Bullen, Alfredo Figueredo, Heinz and Kitty Fischbacher, Don and Kathy Gerace, Perry Gnivecki, John Goggin, Charlie Hoffman, Melu Holdom, Dame Doris Johnson, Bill Keegan, David Knowles, Anne and Jim Lawlor, Ian Lothian, Jim MacLaury, Lady Eunice Oakes, Kim Outten, Froelich Rainey, Bill and Patty Roker, Richard Rose, Ben Rouse, Gail Saunders, Bill Sears, Edward and Lady Henrietta St. George, Sean Sullivan, Grace Turner, John Winter, Ruth Durlacher Wolper, and many others (all colleagues in the field of Lucayan and general Antillean research) have all patiently listened to elements of the hypothesis as it grew, and I am forever in the debt of all these good friends and colleagues.

I am most grateful to Patricia Lewis, Gary Vescelius's widow, and to Tom Vescelius, his son, not only for permission to use Gary's notes and to publish the results of our joint work on Antillean linguistics, but, most importantly, for their enthusiasm in seeing this venture come to fruition for the benefit of other Antillean scholars.

The volume has particularly profited from the insightful, astute, and reasoned editing of Judith Knight of the University of Alabama Press, and of Sue Breckenridge, my copyeditor. Without their common sense and logic, it is doubtful that the book would have emerged from the gestation stage, and I thank them greatly for their forbearance, kindness, and, especially, that intelligent common sense.

Languages of the Pre-Columbian Antilles

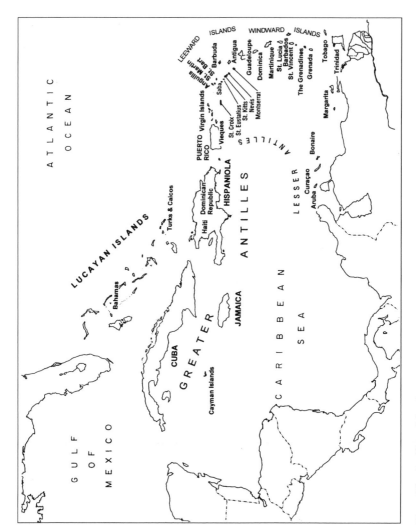

Fig. 1. The Antillean Islands

1

The Pre-Columbian Antilles
An Overview of Research and Sources

The Caribbean Antilles have been home to a kaleidoscopic series of human societies since 4000 B.C. To most people, the very word 'Antilles' summons up visions of heavily jungled, mountainous islands jutting from sapphire seas under azure skies, lulled by the waves which lap their sandy shores, or of serene low-lying atoll-like isles, their beaches covered in forests of swaying coconut palms. Those from less fortunate climes have looked at the Antilles as they looked at the Pacific, as Edens, in which staying alive is the simplest of endeavors and in which work as work is an alien concept. The stepping-stone arc of the Antilles, spanning the eastern Caribbean from Venezuela to Florida, does have some of the most ruggedly mountainous rain forests on earth as well as some of the world's most beautiful beaches, and the outsider's vision is indeed geographically and environmentally accurate, but the rest of the vision is woefully off the mark, for Antillean peoples, again like the peoples of the Pacific islands, have found their homeland beneficent at times and fraught with the usual dangers of everyday life at others. Geography has played a role in forging the fabric of Antillean life, but, as elsewhere, it has been the human factor which has framed the events of history.

Crucial to a definition of history is language, one of the most obvious facets of all human lifeways, for all our thoughts and deeds are, sooner or later, expressed and implemented verbally. Any approach to portrayal of a people, who they are and where they came from, must eventually take into account the language they use, its nature, its structure, and its source and development, but the approach must also take into account the customs and mores the people exhibit and the artifacts they make. We can describe the artifacts dispassionately, and we can through archaeology define the ways in which they are distributed in space and time, gaining a vast amount of inferential information about the implementation of the customs which underlie such artifactual activity. But artifactual data is usually not enough in itself to provide a full picture of a people's lifeways, particularly if those people no longer exist or have been so changed through the passage of time that they no longer practice the lifeways they once had.

This is the situation in the Caribbean Antilles, for though the lifeblood of earlier peoples does indeed flow through the veins of present-day Antillean peoples, with rare exceptions their earlier cultures and languages have disappeared over the passage of time, and it is not possible to extrapolate from the present toward the prehistoric past. Generations of historians, ethnohistorians, and archaeologists have worked toward a definition and description of the pre-Columbian peoples of the Antilles, using documentary evidence from the period of initial contact between the native peoples and Europeans and the large amounts of data gathered laboriously by the spade from archaeological sites. The emergent picture is increasingly more refined and focused, and it will become yet more so in the future, but relying on ethnohistoric and archaeological data alone still allows some of the more puzzling problems of lifeway characterization and explanation to persist.

Among these problems is that of origin—where did the peoples of the Antilles come from, and when and how did they reach their ultimate island destinations? Once there, how did they interact with one another, and why did they interact in the ways that they did? Archaeological and ethnohistorical data have given us partial answers and some very good hints, but language data has only rarely been brought to bear, and professional linguists have only infrequently coupled their knowledge and data with that of archaeologists, ethnologists, and historians, for until recently fewer than half a dozen linguists have been interested in that part of the world, and only two archaeologists practicing in the Caribbean arena have purposely trained themselves in the niceties of both archaeological and linguistic data-gathering, synthesis, and analysis. The same is, of course, true of many other parts of the world, but the fact of the present-day academic separation of the subdisciplines of anthropology does affect problem-resolution in instances of this kind. There is a great need today both for closer cooperation between ethnologists, linguists, and archaeologists in the examination of no longer extant societies and for cross-disciplinary training of new professionals in the field, something which was required until the 1950s in anthropology but, regrettably, is no longer the academic norm.

It is for these reasons that the present book was written—not as a description of the languages of the Antillean peoples, though some has been provided for the lesser-known languages, but as the presentation of added data which may help elucidate the origins and movements of peoples within the archipelago. For that reason, it is also necessary to put such a presentation in its perspective with other work, primarily archaeological, which has been done and which is ongoing in the Caribbean region today. This summation may be of particular use to the reader who is unfamiliar with pre-Columbian Caribbean research and who wishes to garner additional information from other published sources of archaeological, linguistic, and ethnohistorical data. It is also hoped that it will not appear too simplistic to the professional in the field.

There is a great amount of published contemporary documentation as well as unpublished archival information from the time of European contact, 1492 through the 1700s, primarily in Spanish and French, but also in English and Dutch. Unfortunately perhaps, very little has been translated into English, and the serious researcher must regrettably learn to read sixteenth-century Spanish and seventeenth-century French and Dutch with some fluency in order to be able to work from these sources effectively. The major works are those of Bartolomé de Las Casas (1875, 1909, 1951), Ramón Pané (Arrom 1974), and Gonzalo Fernández de Oviedo y Valdez (1851) in Spanish and Raymond Breton (1647, 1665, 1666, 1667) in French. These are all listed in the References section of this volume.

Of easier access to the general reader are the substantive studies on the prehistory of the Antilles, which are usually quite accessible in larger libraries. Again a reading knowledge of at least Spanish, French, and Dutch in addition to English is helpful, though not absolutely necessary.

Interest in the Antillean pre-Columbian past did not really show itself until the year 1876, when *Naturaleza y Civilización de la Gradiosa Isla de Cuba,* the work of Miguel Rodríguez Ferrer, an amateur Cuban archaeologist, was published. It was not, however, until the early 1900s that professional archaeologists, at first largely from the United States but increasingly from Caribbean and Latin American countries as well, began to interest themselves seriously in Caribbean research. Of these, the first and most important was Jesse Walter Fewkes of the Smithsonian Institution, whose work *The Aborigines of Puerto Rico and the Neighboring Islands* was published in 1907. This and his other publications still have value almost a century later. In 1921 M. R. Harrington's *Cuba before Columbus* was published by the Heye Museum of the American Indian in New York, further defining the pre-Columbian cultures of the Antilles, and in 1935 Sven Lovén's *Origin of the Tainan Culture, West Indies* was published. Those three volumes set the stage for subsequent archaeological work in the area, for all of the important questions which needed clarification and resolution were discussed at length in these volumes.

This burgeoning interest was continued during the following decades and strongly reinforced by the decision of the New York Academy of Sciences in the 1930–1940s to fund an archaeological survey of Puerto Rico and the Virgin Islands, led by Froelich Rainey and Irving Rouse, which culminated in the publication of an extremely thorough, well-done four-volume final report (Rainey 1940, 1952; Rouse 1952). That project almost single-handedly stimulated sufficient academic interest in Antillean pre-Columbian research that a number of prestigious universities and museums, led by Yale, began to train graduate students specifically in Caribbean archaeology. During the period from 1940 through the 1960s the number of PhD candidates submitting dissertations in the field of Antillean archaeology more than quadrupled, and by the 1960–1970s a significant number of professional associations devoting themselves largely or exclusively to Antillean research were founded, including particularly the Centro de Estudios Avanzados de Puerto Rico y el Caribe, the Fundación de Historia y Arqueología, and the Center for Archaeological Research in Puerto Rico, the Museo del Hombre Dominicano in the Dominican Republic, the Virgin Islands Archaeological Society, the Musée Régional d'Histoire et d'Ethnographie in Martinique, the Service Regional de l'Archéologie in Guadeloupe, the Institute of Man in Jamaica, the Bahamas Historical Society, the Centro de Antropología and the Instituto de Arqueología of the Academia de Ciencias de Cuba in Havana, and similar institutions in Antigua, Haiti, Curaçao, and elsewhere. These institutions increasingly funded or conducted archaeological site surveys and serious professional excavation throughout the Caribbean and are still very active at the present.

The result of such a surge in professional interest in the Antilles has been an ongoing series of important publications from the 1950s to the present, including articles in professional journals as well as individual monographs and books, on archaeological research and investigation on almost all of the islands of the Caribbean. Chief among these publications is Irving Rouse's 1992 book *The Tainos: Rise and Decline of the People Who Greeted Columbus,* which summarizes Antillean pre-Columbian research from the earliest days of the last century to the present in a manner comparable to that of Sven Lovén's 1935 *Origins of the Tainan Culture, West Indies.* A second important volume, extending the coverage of Rouse's book and summarizing current research to the year 1997, is *The Indigenous People of the Caribbean,* edited by Samuel Wilson.

Accompanying these excellent coverages between the early 1940s and the present are literally hundreds of technical articles on site surveys, excavation reports, and data analysis in the professional journals, the most important of which are, in English, *American Antiquity* in the United States and *Antiquity* in Great Britain, and, in French, the *Journal de la Société des Américanistes* in France. Many of these articles stem from presentations of data at the two most important regular get-togethers of Caribbean archaeologists, the Congress of the International Association for Caribbean Archaeology (Alegría 1993) and the International Congress for the Study of Pre-Columbian Cultures of the Lesser Antilles. Both Congresses bring together most of the practicing professionals in Caribbean archaeology on a regular basis for the reading of data-based papers and the comparison of interpretations and opinions on every facet of the prehistory of the region. The papers presented at these conferences are always published and readily available to the interested reader at any large public or university library.

Only very recently, within the past several decades, has professional work in historical archaeology been undertaken in the Antilles, but that field, too, is gaining rapid momentum and both accomplishing rapid miracles of data recovery and interpretation and in relating the pre-Columbian native American past in those islands to the European and African present through the study of what is known as Contact Period archaeology. An excellent very recent volume on this topic, which should at least be looked at by anyone interested in the Antillean past, is *Island Lives: Historical Archaeologies of the Caribbean* (2001), edited by Paul Farnsworth.

Besides this growing number of well-researched papers and monographs on Antillean archaeology and archaeologically defined prehistory, little has been published during the past century on other aspects of pre-Columbian Antillean cultures. There has been only one substantive work on Taíno ethnohistory, by José Guarch of the Academia de Ciencias de Cuba (Guarch Delmonte 1973). There have also been some excellent ethnographic works on the Taíno religious system (or what we would call a religious system, though it is moot whether the practitioners would have thought of it as a belief system separated from the other aspects of their lives). Antonio M. Stevens-Arroyo's *Cave of the Jagua*, published in 1988, is by far the most thorough study in English, and José Juan Arrom's commentary on the writings of Fr. Ramón Pané (Arrom 1974) is the most thorough study in Spanish. José Oliver (1992a, 1992b, 1993, 1997), Henry Petitjean-Roget (1997a, 1997b), and Miguel Rodríguez (1997) have written important papers on the topic as well. Bill Keegan and M. D. Maclachlan have written on the putative kinship and political system of the Taíno (Keegan and Maclachlan 1989), though their interpretations are based on such tenuous data as to render their final statements more a hypothesis than the empirically demonstrated theory they consider it to be. Publication on the languages of the Antilles, not including a number of articles by researchers untrained in the techniques of data interpretation and analysis of modern linguistics, has been limited to the work of a single professional, the late Douglas Taylor of Dominica, and, with the exception of two articles, been devoted to strictly descriptive materials (Taylor 1951a, 1951b, 1953, 1954, 1955, 1956a, 1956b, 1977). The two exceptions are an article co-authored by Taylor and Berend Hoff, a Dutch specialist on Carib languages on the Island Carib "Men's Language" (Taylor and Hoff 1980), and an article co-authored with Irving Rouse on the correlation of linguistic and archaeological data to determine time-depth in the West Indies (Taylor and Rouse 1955). Additionally, two full studies have been published on Antillean languages—C. H. De Goeje's *Nouvelle Examen des Langues des Antilles* (1939), and Douglas Taylor's *Languages of the West Indies* (1977). Both volumes, while containing a vast amount of well-organized data, concern themselves with an examination of the languages themselves.

Thus Caribbean pre-Columbian research in general and Antillean pre-Columbian research in particular have been largely—at least 98 percent—focused on the gathering of archaeological data and its relatively isolated analysis and interpretation. While this has produced excellent, highly important results, as pointed out earlier, thorough comparative ethnographic-archaeological studies remain to be carried out, as do comparative linguistic-archaeological studies.

A beginning point for such studies could and should be what might be called a concordance of the works of the Spanish, French, Dutch, and English chroniclers, listing every item and event discussed in a cross-referenced index. This onerous, complex, and time-consuming task has yet to be undertaken, though the junior author of this volume had begun such work some years before his death. Once completed, such a concordance should be correlated, item by item, with our known archaeological and linguistic data. Then, and probably only then, will we begin to have a truly balanced view of the data of the Antillean past. From that data should emerge a coherent view of all the facets of the lives of the pre-Columbian Antillean peoples, and most of the interpretive problems still confronting us today might be resolved.

So it is hoped that readers will bear with the unanswered questions many of the chapters in the present volume will leave in their minds, and that they will find some possible clues toward solutions of origin problems in the language data and the suggested archaeological correlations provided here. Readers should bear constantly in mind that what is being written about here provides a *hypothesis,* a data-based guess, not what in science is called a *theory,* a fully substantiated set of facts based on years of satisfactory data-checks. The present volume provides a beginning, not an end, to language and archaeology studies of the pre-Columbian Antilles.

The Languages of the Greater Antilles
A Documentary View

In referring to the Greater Antillean islands of Puerto Rico, Hispaniola, Cuba, and Jamaica, Bartolomé de Las Casas, primary sixteenth-century chronicler of the Indies, reiterates many times in his epochal *Historia de las Indias* (1875:I:326, among others) that *"en todas estas islas hablaban una sola lengua"*—"in all these islands they speak a single language." This statement has, out of context, been taken literally to mean that only one language was spoken by all the inhabitants of the Greater Antilles. That assumption has been followed and the phrase uncritically quoted by almost every researcher of Antillean prehistory who has set pen to paper, generation after generation. The only two exceptions that come to mind are Douglas Taylor and Arnold Highfield (Highfield 1993, 1997), both of whom have been aware of the linguistic complexity of Greater Antillean speech.

Las Casas and the other writers of the early 1500s clearly distinguished *four* aboriginal languages in the Greater Antilles, *Taíno, Macorís, Ciguayo,* and *Guanahatabey,* and for two of those—Taíno and Macorís—he noted a number of geographically distinct dialects.

Such blind-faith acceptance of the *una sola lengua* dictum as the delimiter of Greater Antillean aboriginal languages is unquestionably due to the fact that the phrase has with almost no exception been quoted out of context, largely by researchers who have been working from poor English translations, who have not consulted the original Spanish texts, or—strangely very common among non-Hispanic Caribbean specialists until very recent years—who could not read Spanish. This has regrettably led to the perpetuation of a myth quite undeserving of being perpetuated, for when viewed in context in the originals the *una sola lengua* phrase has a meaning totally different than the literalism accorded it.

The language in question is, of course, Classic Taíno, but the contexts more frequently than not add the qualifying phrase *"porque* cuasi [emphasis added]

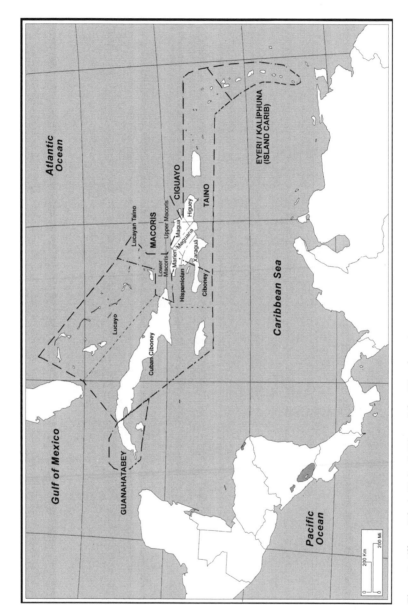

Fig. 2. Antillean Ethnic Units & Hispaniolan Kingdoms in 1492

toda es una lengua y manera de hablar"—"because it is *almost* [italics added] a single language and manner of speech" (e.g., Las Casas 1875:I:291), or the words *universal* or *general* are added—*la lengua universal de toda la tierra* (Las Casas 1875:V:486, for example); *la lengua general desta isla* (Las Casas 1875:V:256).

What emerges from the writings of the times, in other words, is the unambiguous fact that the Taíno language, which had many monolingual speakers and was the numerically dominant language of the Greater Antilles, also served as the *general* language of interchange, *even* with speakers of other languages, serving much the same purpose and for essentially the same reasons as Norman French in post-1066 England. In addition to being the native language of many, it was, in short, a *lingua franca*.

At the time of the Spanish Conquest the five geographical regions of Hispaniola—*Caizcimú, Huhabo, Cayabo, Bainoa,* and *Guacayarima*—were organized into approximately 45 chiefdoms, referred to by the Spanish as "provinces" (Vega 1980). Five of these provinces, *Maguá, Maguana, Higüey, Xaraguá,* and *Marién,* had emerged as dominant. They had become the focal points for five provincial confederations or kingdoms, ruled by the paramount chief of the central province, but with each of its other provincial rulers left with what seem to have been wide local autonomous powers (Vega 1980). These kingdoms, their primary provinces, and selected other provinces of importance to our discussion, are shown on the map in Figure 3.

Puerto Rico, with 20 chiefdoms or provinces, had, for all practical purposes, been organized into a single confederated kingdom, *Borinquen* (*bo-rī-kē*) "The People's Homeland." Cuba, on the other hand, only recently colonized by the Classic Taíno, had no overall political structure above that of the individual settlements. The earlier Cuban natives, the *Ciboney,* Las Casas tells us, had no chiefdoms nor overriding political organization (Las Casas 1875:III:463 *et passim*).

The inhabitants of each of the five Hispaniolan Taíno kingdoms of Maguá, Maguana, Higüey, Xaraguá, and Marién seem to have spoken slightly variant dialects of Classic Taíno, but the *muy más prima* prestige dialect of the Kingdom of Xaraguá, "The Lake Country," in southwestern Hispaniola had assumed the role of second language with most of the population of the Greater Antilles (Las Casas 1875:V:486). It had, as pointed out earlier, become the *lingua franca* of politics, commerce, and culture (Las Casas 1875:I:326)—*"cuya lengua se entendía por toda aquella tierra"* (which language was understood throughout the land) (Pané in Arrom 1974:49). Classic Taíno was certainly the "universal" language of the Indies, but it most decidedly was not the *only* language.

To add to the confusion there have been many listings of putative pre-Columbian Antillean languages by both linguists and non-linguists since the 1500s. Most provide us with the names of well-known attested languages, such

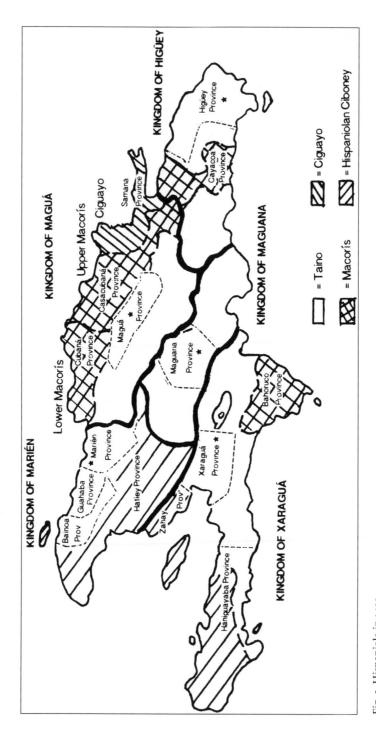

Fig. 3. Hispaniola in 1492

as Taíno, as well as the names of various kinds of erroneous language units, such as a Sub-Taíno language, based on ethno-archaeological data (Mason 1950:210; McQuown 1955:538), or, based on secondary ethnohistoric data, a Ciboney or Guacayarima language (McQuown 1955:522, 525). With only two exceptions (Taylor 1956a, 1977) none were based on even partial examination of the actual documented language data from the primary sources of the 1500s, and even Taylor's listings contain "languages" such as Ciboney, Guacaierima, and Maisi defined from non-language, ethnohistoric data alone (Taylor 1977: 14). Consequently, with due regard for the list-makers, none of them except Taylor's should be taken with any degree of seriousness. While there are, as we shall see, elements of truth in the partial equation of some archaeologically defined groups and some languages or dialects, the equations are not one-to-one, and they do not come from such data-less statements. We need to work from a listing based solely on information supplied by competent, contemporary observers.

Of all the primary sources written between 1492 and 1550 the works of only two authors can be relied upon for such data, because these two were the sole writers in daily, sympathetic contact with native speakers, and they were the only two who understood any of the native languages. These are the works of Bartolomé de Las Casas and Ramón Pané, both missionaries to the Indians—Pané from 1494 to the Lower Macorís and later to the Taíno of Maguá, and Las Casas a resident from 1502 and after his ordination in 1514 a missionary to the Taíno and the Cuban Ciboney. The other chroniclers either never came to the Indies—Anghiera, for example, lived apart from what was left of the native peoples, as did Oviedo—or came after the native cultures and languages had been largely obliterated—Herrera, for example.

This is not to discredit nor dismiss the works of such men. Many, particularly the writings of Anghiera and Oviedo, are of extreme ethnographic and historical importance. There was, however, a significant difference in the kinds of data gathered and methods of collection used by the latter and those used by Las Casas and Pané. Both Las Casas and Pané were meticulous participant-observers very much in the current sense of the term, while Oviedo, Anghiera, and most of the rest were armchair intellectuals, and at times, in the popular tradition of *Amadís de Gaula* and other medieval romances, more than content to supply their readers with second-hand travelogue exotica, regardless of its source, and reveling, it often seems, in the marvelous and the strange. Oviedo in particular was happy to see something totally unique and different in all he saw, especially language data. He is fond of saying that each native community on Hispaniola spoke a totally separate language *"de las quales ninguna se entiende con la otra"* (none of which were mutually intelligible) (Oviedo 1851:I:235).

Las Casas, in particular, had no love for that type of "research," and he is an outspoken critic of its users. "Oviedo," he says, "presumed to write history about what he neither saw nor experienced" (*Oviedo . . . presumió escribir historia de lo que nunca vió, ni cognosció*) (1875:III:23). In a mission report he is even more blunt: "he didn't know what he was talking about" (*mal supo lo que dijo*) (*Colección de Documentos Inéditos de Indias*, 1864–1886:LXIV:57). We know that Las Casas began the writing of his *Historia de las Indias* in 1527, and it has been suggested, with very good logic, that he may, in fact, have done so directly in response to the 1526 publication in Toledo of Oviedo's *Dela natural hystoria delas Indias*, more commonly known as the *Sumario de la Natural Historia de las Indias* (Wilson 1990:9, though Wilson erroneously says this was in response to Oviedo's *Historia General*, the first part of which was actually not published until September 1535 in Seville—see Turner 1985:2). This suggestion, though undocumented, makes very good sense and would be in keeping with Las Casas's strong feelings both about accurate research in general and about Oviedo in particular.

It should, in all fairness, be added that academic and professional jealousy was as rampant then as it is now. The only one who seems to have been exempt was Anghiera, who, as Court Chaplain to Their Catholic Majesties, tutor to the royal children, member of the Council of the Indies, and Official Chronicler of both Castile and the Indies at an annual salary of 80,000 *maravedíes*, perhaps had no reason for jealousy! Just as Las Casas frequently complained about Oviedo, Oviedo, who actively sought the post of Official Chronicler after Anghiera's death in 1526, as frequently criticized the courtier-historians like Anghiera who wrote from Europe *entre cojines y con pie enjuto* (amid cushions and without getting their feet wet). Despite Las Casas's frequent sharp words about him, Oviedo was an astute observer and did spend many of the years from his arrival in Hispaniola in 1514 until his death there in 1557 writing, in his own fashion, about the local scene (Turner 1985:44). If Las Casas was the Indies' first accuracy-emphasizing Baedeker, Oviedo was its popularizing local-color-emphasizing Fodor.

Las Casas and Pané are thus our only fully credible witnesses, and they tell us in considerable detail about all the languages of the Greater Antilles, with some data on the then more poorly known Lesser Antillean speech. The picture painted is described in Table 1 and shown graphically on Figure 4, with all languages and dialects well documented except those indicated by (?).

The primary documentation for the presence of Taíno, Macorís, and Ciguayo on Hispaniola is Las Casas's statement that:

There used to be three distinct, mutually unintelligible languages on this island. One was that of the people we called the Lower Macorís, and the second that of the neighbors of the Upper Macorís [i.e., the Ciguayo], whom we listed above as the fourth and sixth provinces. The other language was universal to the entire country and was the most elegant, with the largest vocabulary and the sweetest sounding. Of the latter the speech of Xaraguá, as I have said earlier, carried the greatest prestige and was the main dialect. (Las Casas 1875:V:486)

[*Tres lenguas había en esta Isla distintas, que la una a la otra no se entendía; la una era de la gente que llamábamos del Macorix de abajo, y la otra de los vecinos del Macorix de arriba, que pusimos arriba por cuarta y por sexta provincias; la otra lengua fué la universal de toda la tierra, y esta era la más elegante y más copiosa de vocablos, y más dulce el sonido; en esto la de Xaraguá, como dije arriba, en todo llevaba ventaja y era muy más prima.*]

Nothing could be much clearer. Las Casas's "second language," as we shall see, is identified in other contexts as Ciguayo.

In his *Apologética Historia* (1909: Chap. 120) Las Casas adds the following about the Hispaniolan languages and about Ramón Pané:

Fray Ramón [Pané] worked as much as he could to learn the three languages that there were on this island, but he only knew that of a small province which, as we have said, was called Lower Macorís, and that one not perfectly. Of the universal language he knew only a little, like the rest of us, although more than most, since no priest, brother, nor lay person knew any of them perfectly except possibly a priest from Palos or Moguer, named Cristóbal Rodríguez, and I think even he didn't know everything about the common language. (Las Casas 1909:Chapter 120)

[*Este fray Ramón escudriñó lo que pudo, según lo que alcanzó de las lenguas que fueron tres las que había en esta isla; pero no supo sino la una de una chica provincia que arriba digamos llamarse Macorix de abajo, y aquélla no perfectamente, y de la universal supo no mucho, como los demás, aunque más que otros, porque negún clérigo, ni fraile, ni segular, supo ninguna perfectamente dellas si no fué un clérigo de Palos o de Moguer, que se llamó Cristóbal Rodríguez, la lengua, y éste no creo penetró del todo la que supo, que fué la común.*]

In specifically distinguishing Macorís from Taíno Las Casas adds:

it was called Macorís in the more wide-spread language of the Indians of this island, like a foreign and barbarous language, because the universal language was more polished and regular or clear. (Las Casas 1875:II:120)

[*decíase Macorix en la lengua de los indios más universal de esta isla, cuasi*

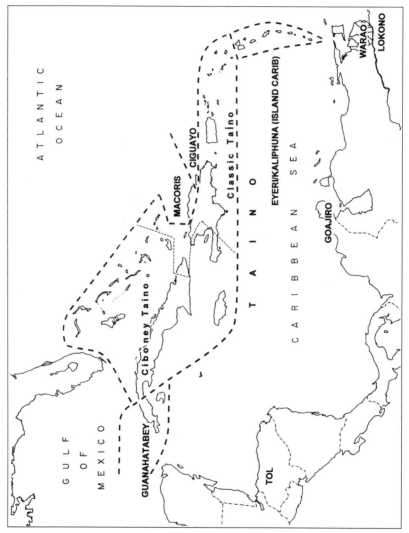

Fig. 4. Antillean Languages in 1492 (From Las Casas & Pané)

Table 1. Antillean Languages in 1492 (From Las Casas and Pané)

All entries except those marked with (?) are documented by Las Casas (1875) and/or Pané (Arrom 1974). Those marked with (?) represent data-based opinion, discussed in the body of the text

Family	Language	Dialect	Location
Arawakan	Taíno	Classic Taíno	1. CUBA: The Cape Maisí region of Oriente Province and sporadically to the west at least as the language of commerce.
			2. HISPANIOLA: East of the Haitian mountains and south of the Río Yaque del Norte in Higüey, Maguana, southern Maguá, and eastern Xaraguá and in the chief towns of Marién.
			3. LUCAYAN ISLANDS: Turks and Caicos only.
			4. PUERTO RICO
			5. LESSER ANTILLES: Vieques, Culebra, St. Croix, and the Leeward Islands except Guadeloupe.
		Ciboney Taíno	1. CUBA: From western Oriente Province westward through Habana Province.
			2. HISPANIOLA: The bulk of Marién and western Xaraguá (modern Haiti).
			3. JAMAICA (?)
			4. LUCAYAN ISLANDS: All islands except the Turks and Caicos.
	Eyeri/ Kaliphuna		LESSER ANTILLES: Guadeloupe in the Leeward Islands and all of the Windward Islands from Dominica south through Grenada.
Waroid (?)	Macorís	Lower Macorís	HISPANIOLA: Northwestern Maguá from Monte Cristi to Puerto Plata, from the coast inland to the vicinity of Santiago.
		Upper Macorís	1. HISPANIOLA: The north-central coast of Maguá from Puerto Plata to Nagua and inland at least as far as San Francisco de Macorís.
			2. HISPANIOLA: The southeast coast around the town of San Pedro de Macorís in former Cayacoa Province of Higüey.
		Guanahatabey (?)	CUBA: Pinar del Río Province and parts of Habana and Matanzas Provinces.
Tolan (?)	Ciguayo		HISPANIOLA: The northeastern coast of Maguá from Nagua south at least to the Río Yuna and eastward through all of the Samaná Peninsula.

como lengua extraña y bárbara, porque la universal era más pulida y regular o clara.]

Las Casas also defines a language difference between Upper and Lower Macorís:

> Having gone past the peaks of Plata, there continues a very high range of mountains like it toward the east. One then comes to the province of Cuhabo, which is Upper Macorís, which we call thus to distinguish it from the Lower Macorís. Macorís means 'foreign language', almost barbarous, because these languages differ both from each other and from the general language of the island. (Las Casas 1875:V:256)
> [*Pasado este monte o sierra de Plata, síguese dél la cordillera de sierras, altísimas como él, hacia el Oriente, i luego está la provincia de Cuhabo, que es el Macorix de arriba, que así lo llamamos a diferencia del de abajo. Macorix quiere decir como lenguaje extraña, cuasi bárbara, porque eran estas lenguas diversas entre si i diferentes de la general desta isla.*]

Macorís, or as Las Casas more usually spells it, *Macorix,* is a Taíno word which means "unfriendly people" (*ma-* 'not' + *ku* 'friend(ly)' = 'unfriendly, alien' + *-ri* 'people.' The lexical form *maku-* occurs in many Arawakan languages in the Guianas with precisely the same meaning and is used to designate non-Arawakan, potentially unfriendly peoples. Even the Arawakan Chané of far southeastern Bolivia use the term *maku* to refer to their non-Arawakan Mataco neighbors across the border in Paraguay. Its use by the Taíno is, therefore, unexceptional, though a clear indication that the peoples to whom it referred were non-Arawakan. The fact that Las Casas (1875:V:486) refers to *three* distinct and mutually unintelligible Hispaniolan languages—Taíno, Macorís, and Ciguayo—not four, would lead one to interpret his statement above as meaning that Lower and Upper Macorís, while different speech forms, were of the order which we would today call dialects rather than separate languages.

Pané, who arrived at La Isabela in Macorís territory on January 2, 1494 (Arrom 1974:4), gives us reinforcement, which is important inasmuch as he had been commissioned explicitly by Columbus to learn the native languages. He provides a lengthy description, telling us that:

> The Admiral then told me that the province of Magdalena or Marolís [Macorís] had a language distinct from the other one, and that it was not understood throughout the country. [For that reason] I should go to live with another leader named Guarionex, a ruler of many people, since his language was understood throughout the land. Thus, by his command, I

went to live with Guarionex. And in truth I said to the Lord Governor Don Christopher Columbus: "Sir, why does Your Grace wish that I go live with Guarionex, since I understand no language except Marolís? Give me permission, Your Grace, to take one of the natives of Nuhuirey with me who have been christianized and understands both languages." He conceded me that request and told me to take whomever I wished with me. (Pané in Arrom 1974:49–50)

[*El señor Almirante me dijo entonces que la provincia de la Magdalena o Marolís tenía lengua distinta de la otra, y que no se entendía el habla por todo el país. Pero que me fuera a vivir con otro cacique principal, llamado Guarionex, señor de mucha gente, pues la lengua de éste se entendía por toda la tierra. Así, por su mandato, fui a vivir con el dicho Guarionex. Y bien es verdad que le dije al señor Gobernador don Cristóbal Colón: "Señor, ¿cómo quiere Vuestra Señoría para que vaya a vivir con Guarionex no sabiendo otra lengua que la de Marolís? Deme licencia Vuestra Señoría para que vaya conmigo alguno de los de Nuhuirey, que después fueron cristianos, y sabían ambas lenguas." Lo cual me concedió, y me dijo que llevase conmigo a quien más me agradase.*]

The distinction between Macorís and Ciguayo is also clearly stated:

It may be noted that a large part of this coast (more than 25 or 30 leagues and a good 15 or even 20 wide, up to the mountains which make a Great Plain of this part of the north) used to be populated by a people called the Macorís, and another called the Ciguayo, and they had *languages* [italics added] different from the general language of the island. (Las Casas 1875:I:434)

[*Es aquí de saber, que un gran pedazo desta costa, bien más de 25 o 30 leguas, y 15 buenas y aún 20 de ancho hasta las sierras que hacen, desta parte del Norte, la gran vega inclusive, era poblado de una gente que se llamaban mazorijes, y otros ciguayos, y tenían **diversas** lenguas* [emphasis added] *de la universal de toda la isla.*]

In a section of the *Historia de las Indias* probably written long after the facts described—between the time the author retired permanently to Spain in 1547 at the age of 73 and his death at age 92 in 1566, a period he devoted to the editing of the work—Las Casas adds the following note regarding the Ciguayo:

I don't remember whether these (the Macorís and the Ciguayo) differed in language, since so many years have passed, and there is no one today from whom the information can be obtained, even though I have spoken many times with people of both generations. It has been more than 50 years—of this at least I am certain—since there have been any Ciguayo where the Admiral now rules. (Las Casas 1875:I:434)

[*No me acuerdo si diferían estos en la lengua (los mazoríges i los ciguayos), como ha tantos años, I no hai hoi uno ni ninguno a quien lo preguntar, puesto que conversé, hartas veces con ambas generaciones, I son pasados ya mas de cincuenta años; esto, al menos, sé de cierto, que los ciguayos, por donde andaba agora el Almirante.*]

The two statements, coming one after the other on the very same page in the *Historia*, seem a bit ambiguous, but the author's statement concerning the presence of three *distinct* languages on the island of Hispaniola (Las Casas 1875:V:486) has substantive lexical evidence, discussed in the next chapter, to support the contention that Ciguayo was related to neither Macorís nor Taíno.

Just as Hispaniola was inhabited by three distinct ethnic entities—the *Taíno*, divided into five kingdoms; the *Macorís*, divided into two distinct provinces, Upper and Lower Macorís; and the *Ciguayo*, on the Samaná Peninsula—each linguistically distinct from the others, so Cuba was also inhabited by three different ethnic groups: the *Guanahatabey* in far western Cuba, the *Cuban Taíno* in far eastern Cuba, and the *Ciboney* in between (see Figure 2). The interplay of ethnic and language units, however, is considerably more difficult to define in Cuba because of the lesser amount of data we have to work with. This is particularly the case in far western Pinar del Río province, the home of the elusive and much-maligned Guanahatabey. Some modern researchers would, in fact, have us perform radical surgery on this particular group from the outset, discounting Governor Diego Velázquez de Cuéllar's 1514 Guanahatabey report to the Crown by saying that "Given the conquistadors' propensity for identifying strange people and places in the New World one should discount that report" and that "the Spanish were not the best ethnographers" (Keegan 1989:377).

The Velázquez report, however, brought the observations of the crew of a Spanish brigantine which had landed on the western end of Cuba to the governor's and the Crown's attention, telling us that:

In the west are the Guaniguaníes and the Guanahatabeyes, who are the westernmost Indians on the island, and the Guanahatabeyes live in the manner of savages, because they have neither houses nor villages nor fields, nor do they eat anything except the meat which they get in the mountains and turtles and fish. (*Colección de Documentos Inéditos de Indias* 1864–1886:VII:35)

[*Poniente están la una se llama Guaniguaníes é la otra Guanahatabeyes, que son los postreros indios dellas; y que la vivienda destos guanahatabeyes es á manera de salvajes, porque no tienen casas ni pueblos, ni labranzas ni comen otra cosa sino las carnes que toman por los montes y tortugas y pescado.*]

While far western Cuba was not penetrated to any great extent until the hispanicization of the late 1600s and 1700s, even by the Taíno so far as we can tell archaeologically (Rouse 1992:20), we are in no position to simply ignore the 1514 Velázquez account, unprofessional and brief though it may seem to some modern-day historians and anthropologists. Columbus's Taíno interpreter, who was given the name Diego Colón, was unable to understand the language of the people who inhabited the shores of the Golfo de Batabanó off the south coast of far western Cuba when that area was reconnoitered in mid-April 1494 during Columbus's second voyage (Rouse 1992:147–148). Las Casas, who was resident on his own *encomienda* at the village of Canareo near the present city of Cienfuegos between 1513 and 1515, states that he had never come into contact with the Guanahatabey, but that he had heard essentially the same information as that contained in the Velázquez report (*Colección de Documentos Inéditos* 1864–1886:XI:424–425). This would seem to preclude any Guanahatabey presence as far east as Las Villas province in west-central Cuba, where Canareo is located. There are also additional sporadic reports of the Guanahatabey through the 1600s, most of them referring to the group as *"de habla distinta"* (of a different language). Toponymic data, discussed in Chapter 7, tends to more than bear out the likelihood that Guanahatabey speech was not Arawakan.

Anghiera added to the problem of Guanahatabey definition by saying that the natives of far western Cuba and those of the southwestern peninsula of Hispaniola, the Guacayarima Peninsula, were the same (Anghiera 1892:II:396–397). Oviedo repeats the same hearsay (Oviedo 1851:I:90). Las Casas, who respected Anghiera as much as he disliked Oviedo, calls all such reports erroneous and incorrect (Las Casas 1875:V:243, 266). He tells us in no uncertain terms that the inhabitants of the province of Haniguayaba, the farthest southwestern province in Xaraguá kingdom on the Guacayarima Peninsula, were no different than those of the rest of that part of Hispaniola, and that the only Guanahatabey-like cave-dwellers were those fleeing the persecution of the Spanish. He adds that the word *guacayarima* simply means 'cape' (*wa-*'country' + *ka-*'far' + *yarima*'end') and refers only to the farthest west cape of Haniguayaba province and was neither the name of a province nor of a people (Las Casas 1875:V:266).

This is important to note inasmuch as almost all researchers have followed Anghiera and Oviedo with regard to both the Guanahatabey and the

"Guacayarima," invariably marking the Guacayarima Peninsula off on the map as a non-Arawak region. This is manifestly incorrect if we follow Las Casas's eyewitness statements and if we follow what archaeological data we have from the region, which supports Las Casas (Rouse 1982).

In Oriente province, at the far eastern end of Cuba directly across the Windward Passage from Hispaniola, the Cuban Taíno dominated the scene. That they were comparative newcomers to the island is quite clear from Las Casas's description:

> on account of the persecution and torment that the people suffered from the Spanish, those who could . . . fled to the island of Cuba . . . and to the region which is nearest the point or cape which they call in their language Maicí. . . . The majority of the people who inhabit the island of Cuba come from and were natives of Hispaniola, for the earlier population of Cuba was like that of the Lucayan Islands, about whom we spoke in Books I and III . . . and they called themselves in their language *Ciboney*. . . . It was later that people from Hispaniola went across to Cuba, mainly after the Spanish began to torment and oppress their neighbors, and once in Cuba they overcame the Cuban natives by peaceful means or force. . . . It has not been fifty years since the Hispaniolans crossed over to Cuba. (Las Casas 1875:III:463 *et passim*)
> [*por las persecuciones y tormentas que . . . las jentes de esta isla (de la Española) de los españoles padecían, los que podían huir . . . se pasaban huyendo a la isla de Cuba . . . y en la tierra que está mas propíncua a la punta o cabo desta isla, que se llamaba en su lengua Maycí. . . . Toda la mas de la gente de que estaba poblada aquella isla (la de Cuba) era pasada y natural desta isla Española, puesto que la mas antigua y natural de aquella isla (de Cuba) era como la de los Lucayos de quien hablamos en el libro I y III . . . y llamábamos en su lengua cibonéyes. Después pasaron desta isla Española alguna gente, mayormente después que los españoles comenzaron a fatigar y a oprimir los vecinos naturales desta, y llegados en aquella, por grado o por fuerza en ella habitaron y sojuzgaron, por ventura los naturales della . . . no había cincuenta años que los desta hobiesen pasado a aquella isla.*]

In the same account Las Casas specifically describes the flight and emigration of the Taíno sub-chief Hatüey of Guahaba province in far northwestern Haiti and most of his people across the 60-some miles of the Windward Passage to the Cabo Maisí region of Oriente province in Cuba, where they settled and lived in peace until the Spanish ultimately arrived, captured him, and burnt him at the stake for his trouble in fleeing their bountiful largesse! The descriptions of a Hispaniolan migration to eastern Cuba, beginning in approximately 1450 if we follow Las Casas's account, would seem to be ethnohistoric documentation for what archaeologists know as the Taíno Chican invasion of far eastern Cuba immediately preceding and during Conquest times (Sullivan 1981). The Hispaniolan Taíno spread, apparently with some rapidity, throughout eastern and central Cuba and had made sporadic settlements as far west as Habana province by the time the Spanish arrived under Governor Diego Velázquez de Cuéllar. The greatest number of settlers, however, seem to have been concentrated in Oriente province and the Cabo Maisí region.

Cuba's primary population, Las Casas's *la mas antigua y natural,* the Ciboney, dominated numerically from western Oriente province on westward through the island to Pinar del Río province in the far west. In his youth Las Casas took part in the Spanish conquest of Cuba and, as mentioned earlier, lived among the Ciboney of west-central Cuba on his *encomienda* at Canareo from 1513 to 1515. He describes their customs in considerable detail (Las Casas 1875:III:463 *et passim*). These descriptions bear no similarity to the little we know of the Guanahatabey. Las Casas notes the many specific differences which set the Ciboney apart from the Hispaniolan and Cuban Taíno, but he notes that "the language of the inhabitants of Cuba and Hispaniola is the same" (*siendo toda una lengua la de los de Cuba y de la Española*) (Las Casas 1875:I:359). There seems no reason to doubt that the Ciboney were speakers of Taíno. There is, however, lexical evidence, discussed in the next chapter, which indicates that Ciboney speech was not Classic Taíno but, rather, a separate dialect, which we shall refer to as *Ciboney Taíno* in contrast to the *Classic Taíno* of Hispaniola. As we shall see later, it was this dialect which was also spoken throughout the Lucayan Islands except for the southernmost Turks and Caicos. This data-based statement is reinforced by Columbus' repeated report that the Indians of the north coast of Cuba understood his Indian guide from the central Bahamas (Columbus in Fuson 1987:100, 103, 107, *et passim*).

Ciboney Taíno, it should be noted, is a language dialect, not a people or an ethnic unit. This dialect of the language was probably spoken by several separate ethnic units—definitely by the Cuban Ciboney and the Lucayo, and probably by the unnamed inhabitants of Jamaica and by many of the more rural inhabitants of western Hispaniola (the present country of Haiti).

The original usage of the terms *Guanahatabey, Ciboney,* and *Taíno*—free from ill-advised equation of the two former and unencumbered by the addition of invented entities such as the Guacayarima—has been normal among Spanish-speaking Antillean scholars until recent years. Among English-speaking specialists, however, as well as the younger generation of Spanish-speaking scholars, who have largely followed the lead of the American specialists, the term *Ciboney* has, like *Guanahatabey,* been applied and misapplied to a plethora of concepts—a nonceramic archaeological culture (Osgood 1942), an ethnohistoric entity equatable with the Guanahatabey (Harrington 1921, Lovén 1935), and a language, presumably non-Taíno and non-Arawakan (Mason 1950:Map). By far the most persistent usage is that which equates the Ciboney and the Guanahatabey, making both nonceramic and non-Arawakan. In this parlance the rest of the native population of Cuba was simply Taíno, those characteristics differentiating it from the Classic Taíno of central Hispaniola constituting the Western Taíno archaeological tradition (originally referred to as the Sub-Taino tradition).

Such confusion clearly stems from the fact that few of the earlier English-speaking scholars bothered to consult any of the original sixteenth-century primary sources—that is, the writings of Las Casas and Pané—but, rather, contented themselves with the long-available English translations of Anghiera and the writings of Oviedo and even later chroniclers such as Herrera. They can not be entirely faulted for this, inasmuch as Las Casas's *Historia de las Indias* was not available even in Spanish until 1875, and Pané's brief document was buried in Ferdinand Columbus's *Historia del Almirante de las Indias* and not readily available in English until Bourne's 1906 translation. Las Casas's widely known *Brevíssima Relación de la Destruyción de las Indias,* available in Spanish since 1552, and his *La Apologética Historia,* available even in English translation since 1656, were traditionally viewed in the early years of this century as lopsided polemics on Spanish atrocities against the Indians—the notorious "Black Legend"—and consequently largely dismissed by most scholars. Nonetheless, the root of the ethnic identification problem stems from English-speaking researchers, scholars who either could not or did not consult the original Spanish primary documents.

The mix-up first appears in Walter Fewkes's *Prehistoric Culture of Cuba* (1904), to be adopted and repeated in Harrington's widely read *Cuba before Columbus* (1921), from whence it was taken up by Sven Lovén in his epochal *Origins of the Tainan Culture, West Indies* (1935), the latter quickly becoming *the* final authority on West Indian prehistory for all English-speaking scholars, quoted from as though it were itself a primary source, frequently treated with an attribution of infallibility embarrassing even to its author.

Following the American lead and Lovén, the confusion gradually spread to the younger Spanish-speaking scholars as well. Ricardo Alegría (1981:5–6) has, however, recently set the record straight again for Spanish speakers, and Irving Rouse (1987:294) has done the same for English speakers. The restored usage, returning to the original sixteenth-century practice of keeping both Guanahatabey and Ciboney separate from each other and from the Cuban and Hispaniolan Taíno, has yet to be used as widely as it ought. At last, however, English-speaking Antillean scholars are nowadays more frequently acquiring at least a reading facility in Spanish, rare in the past, and turning directly to the primary sources rather than their generally poor English translations.

Unfortunately we have neither ethnohistoric nor ethnolinguistic data from the chroniclers on Jamaica, but archaeological data make it clear that the 1492 population of that island was part of what archaeologists have called the Western Taíno tradition (Rouse 1992:7, Figure 3), formerly known, as pointed out earlier, as the Sub-Taíno tradition. It will consequently be hypothesized here that Jamaican speech and culture were probably akin to Cuban Ciboney.

An archaeological site survey of the neighboring Cayman Islands, northwest of Jamaica and due south of the central Cuban coast, in 1922 by Walter Fewkes of the Smithsonian Institution's Bureau of American Ethnology (Fewkes 1922: 258), a second survey of Grand Cayman in 1958 by the senior author of this volume (Granberry 1958), and a third survey of Grand Cayman by Anne V. Stokes in 1990 with a follow-up by Stokes and William F. Keegan of the Florida Museum of Natural History in 1993 (Stokes and Keegan 1998) turned up no evidence of prehistoric occupation of the islands.

Puerto Rico is known to have been both ethnically and linguistically part of the Classic Taíno domain—persistent statements suggesting a non-Arawakan, non-Taíno resident Carib population are discounted by Las Casas, who says unequivocally that "there were never Caribs in Puerto Rico" (*no eran en la isla de San Juan Caribes jamás*) (Las Casas 1909:Chapter 205). To the east of Puerto Rico, in the Virgin Islands and south into the Leeward Islands, probably to but not including Guadeloupe, archaeological research indicates a Taíno presence (Morse 1997:36–45). Just as the Ciboney Taíno–speaking peoples can be distinguished archaeologically from the Classic Taíno, and are hence called the Western Taíno, so the archaeological data from eastern Puerto Rico, Vieques, the Virgin Islands, and the Leeward Islands enable us to distinguish their inhabitants from the Classic Taíno peoples as Eastern Taíno (Rouse 1992:7). An Eastern Taíno presence is indicated archaeologically at least as far south into the Leewards as Saba, where the Kelby Ridge site, dating to about 1300 A.D., clearly represents an outpost of Taíno people (Hofman 1995; Hofman and Hoogland 1991).

In the Windward Islands, from Guadeloupe south through Grenada in the Lesser Antilles and likely extending as far north as sporadic semipermanent settlements on St. Croix, were the *Eyeri*, also called *Iñeri* or, with Anghiera's Italianate spelling, *Igneri* (Taylor 1977:22–28; Figueredo 1987:6). Their probable origins and identity are discussed in Chapter 6. Archaeologically the Lesser Antilles were inhabited from Archaic times and the later influx of Arawakan peoples right up to the time of European contact, and the archaeological data, discussed in Chapter 6, indicate a clear developmental continuity from each successive ceramic-producing Arawakan culture to the next, from the first archaeologically known culture, the Cedrosan Saladoid about 500–200 B.C., through those of the Suazoid tradition, beginning about 1000 A.D. and ending about 1450 (Haag 1965:242–245; Allaire 1977, 1990; Davis and Goodwin 1990). The source of both Greater Antillean and Lesser Antillean Arawakan cultures, as seen archaeologically, is certainly the Cedrosan Saladoid tradition (Rouse 1992:131; Allaire 1991), yet the voluminous language data indicate that the Eyeri language, though Arawakan, was neither identical to nor even closely related to Taíno. Its closest parallels are found in the language of the Lokono Arawak of the Guiana mainland (Taylor 1977:22–28). Thus, while certainly of ultimate common ancestry, the Taíno and Eyeri languages had come to be quite different by the time of European intervention.

The picture is yet more complex, for archaeological data indicate that a major cultural transformation occurred throughout the Windward Islands sometime in the years around 1450 A.D. There are rapid changes in the ceramic record—Eyeri Suazoid wares vanish rather suddenly, to be replaced by other wares, on St. Vincent called Cayo wares (Boomert 1985), and there is a shift in site locations from the drier leeward sides of the islands, favored by the Eyeri, to the wetter windward sides (Allaire 1991). Rouse (1992:130–133), equates these changes with the arrival of the Kalínago or Kalíphuna, a Cariban people of the Guianas, to the islands. The Kalínago/Kalíphuna—a term meaning 'Manioc-Eating People' (see Taylor 1977:25)—began moving into the islands on what were probably at first warring expeditions, but these forays in very short order became long-term colonizing ventures. In a matter of several generations intermarriage between Kalínago Carib men and Eyeri Arawak women gave rise to a new people both physically and culturally—the Island Carib.

If there ever was a poor choice of terms, this is it, for while the Eyeri adopted their conqueror's name, Kalíphuna, a number of Carib artifactual traits, and a limited number of Carib vocabulary items and grammatical conventions into their language, the latter used primarily by the men, the new Kalíphuna people were still by and large Arawakan, and their language, to this day called Garífuna by their Belizean, Guatemalan, and Honduran descendants in Central America, is a latter-day development from Eyeri Arawakan (Breton 1665, 1666, 1667; Hadel 1975; Taylor 1951, 1952, 1953, 1954, 1955, 1956a, 1956b, 1958a, 1958b, 1977; Taylor and Hoff 1980; Taylor and Rouse 1955). Its linguistic history, traced in Chapter 6, is distinct from that of Taíno, and though both languages are members of the Northern Maipuran branch of Arawakan, they were not in 1492 closely related. Both languages originally stemmed from a single Northern Maipuran source in the millennium before the birth of Christ, but Taíno developed to its fifteenth–sixteenth century form in relative isolation in the Greater Antilles, while, to judge from its many similarities and close affinities with Guiana Lokono, Eyeri developed in rather close ongoing contact with its continental relatives during the first 1,400 years of its history.

It is clear, in other words, that two Northern Maipuran Arawakan languages, Taíno and Eyeri-Kalíphuna, mutually unintelligible and not, by 1492, closely related, were the primary native languages of the Greater and Lesser Antilles respectively at the time of Spanish intervention.

In summary, while Taíno was clearly the dominant language of the Greater Antilles and served as a *lingua franca* throughout both that region and its western and eastern peripheries, it did not completely displace two, perhaps three, earlier non-Arawakan languages on those islands: Macorís, in at least two dialects on the northwestern coast and in the northern region of the Vega of Hispaniola respectively; Ciguayo on the Samaná Peninsula on Hispaniola; and, perhaps a separate language, perhaps a dialect of Macorís, Guanahatabey, in Pinar del Río province and parts of Habana and Matanzas provinces in western Cuba. The Ciboney of Cuba were speakers of a Taíno dialect with, as we shall see, its own peculiarities. It is primarily this constellation of languages and its correlates in the archaeological data which will concern us in the remaining chapters of this volume.

3

Anomalous Non-Taíno Language Data from the Greater Antilles

We have over 200 attested Classic Taíno language forms, most of them plant and animal names, social titles, and personal names, along with a half-dozen full sentences and approximately 1,000 analyzable toponyms on which to base a lexical and structural analysis of that language. From internal evidence we can say that Taíno was Arawakan and that together with Eyeri it belonged to the Northern Maipuran branch of the Arawakan language family. We can also say that, like Goajiro, spoken on the Guajira Peninsula in northwestern Venezuela, it was largely a conservative language, retaining some early Northern Maipuran characteristics later lost or altered in most other languages of that branch of Arawakan, including Eyeri and its Island Carib/Garífuna descendant. Like Goajiro it also shows certain unique innovations not shared by other Northern Maipuran tongues.

The linguists' and archaeologists' greatest problem with the ensuing analysis of the known non-Taíno language data will arise from the fact that we have for Guanahatabey only a handful of possible toponyms. For Macorís, presumably the Lower Macorís dialect, we have a single lexical form and another handful of toponyms. For Ciguayo we have only one word and a probable toponym, and for the Ciboney dialect of Taíno we have only one definite word and a number of toponyms. There is additionally a single lexical item from Classic Taíno which is so unique that it will be examined here. Together, these seeming anomalies are hardly the stuff that linguistic empires are made of, for the rules of regular phonological correspondence can hardly be applied to such a miniscule database, nor can much be said about morphological structures on that same base.

Something, however, can occasionally be said about isolated language forms which happen fortuitously to show phonological or morphological peculiarities unique to another known language or group of languages, particularly if the peculiarities belong to languages spoken in the immediate geographical environs of the anomaly users. This is the case with the single surviving Ciguayo word and the single surviving probable Ciguayo toponym (Granberry 1991b).

THE CIGUAYO LANGUAGE DATA

Perhaps not surprisingly, the meaning of the surviving Ciguayo word is 'gold.' Las Casas tells us on three separate occasions that a Ciguayo informant told him that "Here [among the Ciguayo] they don't call gold *caona* [the normal Taíno word] . . . but *tuob*" (*Aquí no llaman caona al oro . . . sino tuob*) (Las Casas 1875:I:282, 326, 434). He goes on to say that the same Indian told Columbus that the word "tuob" was also used on the islands of Matinino and Guanín. This statement, however, was a misunderstanding on the part of Columbus and the Spanish, a misunderstanding recently discussed by Henry Petitjean-Roget in an insightful article entitled "The Taino Vision: A Study in the Exchange of Misunderstanding" (Petitjean-Roget 1997a). As Petitjean-Roget demonstrates, the Indians thought the Spanish were asking for the use and import of the gold ornaments which they wore, not just the name of the substance from which they were made. While the Spanish did learn the native terms for 'gold,' they were also given traditional information on the mythological world from which the ornaments gained their cultural use as protective religious amulets.

The Spanish took such added information literally, and thought of Matinino and Guanín as actual islands on which they would find more gold. In fact, however, these putative islands were but part of the mythical Taíno Otherworld, as Ramón Pané's account of Taíno beliefs indicates (Arrom 1974:24–25), and the word *tuob* was simply the Ciguayo word for the substance from which such protective ornaments were made. As Petitjean-Roget so eloquently says: "faced with the Spaniards' insistence on learning about the origins of gold, the Indians consistently repeated to them the mythical story of the origins of gold ornaments, or guanins. The island of women without men, Matinino, of women covered with copper plaques for protection, that Columbus sought beyond the land of Carib [Puerto Rico], was none other than the island where, in the myth, the hero Guahayona abandoned the women he had seduced" (Petitjean-Roget 1997a:174). Nowhere in the data, from any colonial source, is there reference to the use of the word *tuob* outside a Ciguayo context—it is strictly and uniquely a Ciguayo word.

Las Casas is very careful to tell us which syllable of each newly cited native word bears primary stress, unless the word in question is monosyllabic or conforms to normal Spanish stress rules—on the penultima if the final syllable ends in a vowel, *n*, or *s;* otherwise on the ultima. He makes no stress statement with regard to *tuob,* which indicates that instead of a two-vowel, disyllabic

word, *tu-ob,* it was likely monosyllabic *twób.* Orthographic <u> after a consonant and before another vowel is regularly used in the Spanish of all time periods to render the phonetic *w* of English and other languages, so its presence
in *tuob* is not surprising and its interpretation there as *w* unexceptional.

Twób could not, even in the wildest stretches of linguistic imagination, be
considered a native Arawakan form—Taíno, Eyeri, or otherwise. The normative phonological shape of Arawakan morphemes is CV(CV)—consonant +
vowel, usually monosyllabic, but occasionally a string of such syllables. Also
not infrequent is the shape (V)CV—(vowel) + consonant + vowel, but CCV,
VCC, and (C)CVC simply do not occur. Even words borrowed from languages
which do have consonant clusters or syllables which end in a consonant are
regularized to the Arawakan norm. Thus Island Carib/Garífuna *isúbara* 'cut-
lass' from Spanish *espada,* or *isíbuse* 'mirror' from Spanish *espejo,* for example.
The same CV(CV) norm occurs in all of the Andean-Equatorial and Macro-
Chibchan languages of northern South America (Greenberg 1960). The only
South American language in reasonable proximity to the Caribbean littoral
which does have a CVC norm and also shows the occurrence of consonant clusters is Gê, but the distance is formidable, and there is no lexical form in any of
the Gê languages from which *twób* might convincingly derive.

The closest language stocks which regularly show a CVC closed-syllable
norm are the Mayan languages of Yucatán and Guatemala and the Tolan
(Jicaque) languages of central and northern Honduras. The Proto-Cholan
Maya form **tun* 'stone' with pluralizing morpheme **-ob^i,* to yield a putative
tu(n)ob^i 'stones,' certainly comes immediately to mind (Kaufman and Norman
1984:91, 133), but no Mayan language uses form-initial C+*w,* and there would
remain the problem of explaining away the morpheme-final *-n* of **tun.* The
C+*w* phenomenon does, however, occur in Eastern Tol, in which the only al-
lowable syllable-initial consonant cluster is in fact a consonant followed by
semivowel *w* or *y* (Fleming and Dennis 1977:122). In that environment infixed
semivowels serve specific verbal or nominal functions. With nouns a *-w-* infix indicates third-person possession and *-y-* second-person possession (Holt
1999:35–36), the infix coming between the initial consonant and first vowel
of the form, as in *p^{h}el* 'arm,' *p^{h}wel* 'his arm' (Dennis and Dennis 1983:58), or
kom 'liver,' *kyom* 'your liver' (Fleming and Dennis 1977:122). Such possessed
nouns, that is, take the phonological form CwCV, the precise phonological
shape of *twób.*

The Tolan languages—extinct Western or El Palmar Tol and surviving Eastern Tol or Jicaque—are likely Hokan languages (Holt 1999:5, Langdon 1979:593),
related to a spectrum of tongues from Oaxaca in southern Mexico up the
Pacific coast as far as northern California and Oregon. Pomo in coastal central
California and the Yuman languages of southern California, Arizona, and Baja

California are perhaps the most well known. The Yurumango language of the Pacific coast of Colombia may also be Hokan (Greenberg 1960). The authors are, of course, well aware of the "catchall" character of both the doggedly stuck-to Hokan and Penutian language macrophyla. We would, however, agree with those who see at least a core of linguistic reality in both phyla, despite the inclusion over the years of a good many unlikely candidates for membership. It is generally clear that whatever reality Hokan has, it represents a very early language stratum in the Americas, one whose languages have frequently been replaced or displaced later in time to their present disparate locations by speakers of other languages.

If Tolan is indeed Hokan, and if the peculiarities of the CwVC normative form are meaningful, both of which are, of course, open to various views depending upon one's feelings about application of the principles of the comparative method, then *twób* not only fits the expected phonological pattern, but it also has a convincing etymology and morphological patterning strikingly similar to those of the Hokan languages.

The word for 'stone, rock' is *pe* in Eastern Tol (Fleming and Dennis 1977:122), *be* in Western Tol (Conzemius 1922:166), enabling us to reconstruct Proto-Tol *pe* (Campbell 1979:967). This form is coordinate with the Hokan Chontal of Oaxaca (Tequistlatec) form -*bik,* which has the same meaning.

For Hokan languages further to the north, Langdon (1979:636–639) presents her Proto-Yuman reconstructions along with Proto-Pomo reconstructions by Sally McLendon and Robert Oswalt and additional material from Yuman Diegueño. Proto-Pomo has di-morphemic *$q^h a^{\prime}$-be* or *$q^h a^{\prime}$-bé* 'stone, rock,' while Proto-Yuman has *$^{\prime}$-wi(:)(y)*, and Diegueño *$^{\prime}$ə-wiľ*. The primary base morpheme of these di-morphemic forms is the second morpheme, -*be*, -*bé*, -*wi(:)(y)*, or -*wiľ*, which means 'stone, rock.' Comparison of the proto-forms indicates that the morpheme consists of a bilabial *b* or *w* plus a mid-to-high front vowel *e* or *i*. The bilabial is always voiced *b* or *w*, not a voiceless *p*, as evidenced for Proto-Tol (Campbell 1977:967). The basic Hokan root would seem, therefore, to have been either *be*, *we*, *bi*, or *wi*.

The initial morpheme in the Proto-Pomo forms, *$q^h a^{\prime}$-*, also occurs as *$q^h ah$-* in Proto-Pomo * $q^h ah$-ca* or * $q^h ah$-ká* 'flint,' taking the shape *$^{\prime}ah$-* in the Yana form *$^{\prime}ah$-$k^w a$,* 'metal.' That is, Hokan words for specific kinds of stone and ores use a base meaning 'stone, rock' preceded by a form-initial morpheme which identifies the particular characteristics of the stone in question. Thus *$q^h a^{\prime}$-* and its variants seem to refer to 'flint or metal-bearing ores.'

On the Hokan analogy, the crucial morpheme of Ciguayo *twób* would be the lexeme-final morpheme -*b(e)* 'stone, rock.' The lack of the final *e* might reflect a phonological phenomenon not infrequent in many languages and specifically present in Eastern Tol; namely, unstressed vowels tend to be reduced to phonetic schwa (ə), as in English 'bʌt' (Fleming and Dennis 1977:127). Since Tol lexemes ending in a vowel bear stress on the penultimate vowel (Fleming and Dennis 1977:127), the final *e* of what was originally *twóbe* would bear weak stress and would consequently take the form *twóbə*. Since such mid-central vowels did not exist phonemically in sixteenth-century Spanish, nor do they in modern Spanish, it is unlikely that such an *uh* sound would have been indicated in Las Casas's orthography.

Pressing the Hokan analogy further, the Ciguayo *-b(e)* 'stone' morpheme may be preceded by an infix morpheme *-w-*, related to Eastern Tol noun-indicating possessive infix *-w-* 'its.' The other morpheme in the Ciguayo form, word-initial *to-*, should, by analogy with broader Hokan, describe some special quality of the 'stone' in question. There is, in fact, an Eastern Tol morpheme *tɨ*, which means 'heavy' (Dennis and Dennis 1983:39). Ciguayo *twób(e)* 'gold,' on analogy with Honduran Tolan and other Hokan languages, in short, might have meant 'heavy stone'—*to-* 'heaviness' + *-w-* 'its' + *-b(ə)* 'stone'—a not unlikely designation for gold ore. Is this reaching? It may be. The analysis, however, is certainly possible phonologically, morphologically, and semologically without breaking any of the norms of Tol and general Hokan word formation.

Anghiera gives us the only other surviving word, a toponym, which probably belonged to what seems to have been the once more wide-spread Ciguayo tongue. He says: "The names which the original inhabitants gave to Hispaniola, were first *Quizquella*, later Haití, not only just because as a decision of those who gave the name, but because of the effect that the names created . . . *Quizquella* means great size" (*Los nombres que los primeros habitantes pusieron à la Española, fueron primero Quizquella, después Haití, y no sólo por voluntad de los que le pusieron el nombre, sino por el efecto que ellos creían. . . . Quizquella la interpretan grandeza*) (Anghiera 1892:II:384).

Like *tuob*, the toponym *Quizquella*, phonetically *kʰiskʰeya*, could not, because of its phonological shape, be a Taíno form. The consonantal cluster *-skʰ-* would not occur in any native Taíno form. Anghiera goes on to describe the word as indicating extreme magnitude in size *"por el aspecto áspero de sus montañas y la negra espesura de sus bosques"* (because of the harsh [= rough and dry] aspect of its mountains and the dark denseness of its forests). As with *tuob*, there is a Tol word which matches the name *Kʰiskʰeya* both phonologically and semologically, namely the form *kʰisyana* with the meaning 'very mountainous' (Dennis and Dennis 1983:I:35; II:28). The base form of that word is *kʰis*, which means 'obsidian, very hard rock' (Dennis and Dennis 1983:I:35). The morpheme *-ya* may be related to the Tol word for 'tree,' *yo* (Dennis and Dennis 1983:I:51). Morpheme *-na* is possibly a reflex of the Tol objective suffix, which frequently takes the form *-n* (Holt 1999:37–38). The second syllable of *Kʰiskʰeya*, *-kʰe-*, is probably a partial reduplication of the initial syllable, a process often used with nouns in Tol to indicate not just plurality but a proliferating multiplicity (Holt 1999:38–39). Thus, the word which Anghiera translates as *grandeza,* particularly given his lengthy description of what it implied, may have meant 'a very mountainous, heavily forested terrain.' While again perhaps a stretch to some, particularly since we are comparing language data separated by 500 years, the phonological, morphological, and semological match of Quizquella *K^hisk^heya* and *k^hisyana* to 'very mountainous' is rather remarkable and particularly appropriate given the terrain of the western half of Hispaniola.

If indeed Ciguayo was the latter-day remnant of a once more wide-spread Tolan language in the Greater Antilles, when did its speakers reach those islands from the Central American mainland? The archaeological correlates will be discussed in the next chapter, but for our purposes here linguistic data alone are revealing. Lyle Campbell (1979:919) estimates glottochronological time-depth for the separation of now extinct Western El Palmar Tol from surviving Eastern Tol at approximately 1,000–1,600 years. The phonological and morphemic parallels between reconstructed Proto-Tol (Campbell 1979:966–967) and Ciguayo, while close, are parallels, not identities. We are therefore likely talking about a time depth some thousands of years or more before Proto-Tol as the time of separation of an early Proto-Tol on the one hand and Ciguayo on the other from general Proto-Tolan. On this basis it may be postulated that Tolan speakers could not have arrived in the Greater Antilles much later than 3,000 B.C., perhaps much earlier. Nonetheless, our earlier caution needs to be repeated—the accuracy of any comparative statement based on only two lexical items is by nature both logically suspect and uncertain.

THE MACORÍS LANGUAGE DATA

As with Ciguayo, so with Macorís there is only one lexical form explicitly identified in the documentary sources as coming from that language. This is the word *baeza,* glossed as 'no.' Las Casas says "In that language called Macorís, which we indicated earlier was different from the general language, they say *baeza* for 'no'" (*Item, en la lengua que dejimos arriba que había fuera de la general, que se llamaba el Macorix, se decía baeza, por no*) (Las Casas 1909:633).

This word is of rather obvious Arawakan origin, though interestingly of neither Taíno nor Eyeri derivation. The general privative-negative prefix of Arawakan languages is *ma-*. This is the reconstructed Proto-Maipuran form (Payne 1990:77) and also the form which occurs in both Taíno (Taylor 1977:19) and Eyeri/Island Carib (Taylor 1952:150). In most other Northern Maipuran languages the prefix also takes the same shape—Manao *ma-esa* 'no, not,' for example. Only rarely, as in Amarakaeri, a Pre-Andine Arawakan language of the Pilcopata River region in Peru, does the prefix take the form *ba-* (Payne 1990:77).

The second morpheme of the Macorís word *baeza, -ésa,* also occurs in many Arawakan languages, Maipuran and non-Maipuran, with the structural meaning of 'counter, number, thing.' It is often found as part of a morpheme-string in numbers, regardless of the number in question. In Northern Maipuran, however, its usual phonological shape is -*Vti,* where *V* stands for any vowel; thus, in Taíno *héketi* 'one,' Lokono *bíbiti* 'four,' and Machiguenga *pitati* 'two' and *mawati* 'three.' The lexical meaning of forms containing the counter morpheme is 'one thing,' 'two things,' 'three things,' and so on; thus, Manao *ma-esa* means 'no thing = nothing = not,' and presumably the Macorís form, which would phonetically be *ba-ésa* also meant 'no thing = nothing.'

Just as *ma-* rather than *ba-* is the usual phonetic shape for the privative-negative morpheme in Northern Maipuran, so -*Vti* is the usual counter morpheme form, not-*ésa,* despite the fact that it occurs in Manao and a few other Northern Maipuran languages. One would expect something like *ma-ti* as the form for 'nothing' in most Northern Maipuran languages, not *ba-ésa.* Generally forms of the counter morpheme with sibilant *s* or an affricate *ts* rather than stop *t* are more frequent in the Eastern Maipuran languages, particularly those near the headwaters of the Xingú and Tapajós Rivers in Brazil—Mehinacú *ah-itza* 'not,' Waurá *a-itza* 'not,' Paresís *ma-isa* 'not.'

Such data makes a Taíno, Eyeri, or general Northern Maipuran source for Macorís *ba-ésa* highly improbable. If this is the case, then resolution of the problem of its origin is not simple. One would have to postulate the presence of another, non-Taíno, non-Eyeri but still Arawakan people on Hispaniola at some time in the past, one whose source was, to judge from those Arawakan languages with negative words like Macorís *baeza,* south and east of the Northern Maipuran heartland, perhaps somewhere on the extreme southern sections of the Guiana coast.

This in fact is exactly what the archaeologists Marcio Veloz Maggiolo, Elpidio Ortega, and Ángel Caba Fuentes have postulated on archaeological grounds alone (1981:393–397). The archaeological peculiarities of the northwestern and north-central coast of Hispaniola, extending down into the Vega, have long been noted, particularly the distinctive Meillacan pottery wares and the use of the *montículo y várzea* (river-bank mound) method for the wet-cultivation of manioc. The distribution of these characteristics coincides with ethnic Macorís territory (Veloz Maggiolo, Ortega, and Caba Fuentes 1981). Because the sources of manioc wet-cultivation and certain characteristics of Meillacan pottery can not be traced to Taíno origins, Veloz Maggiolo, Ortega, and Caba Fuentes suggest that they may be the result of a migration of a non-Taíno Arawakan people directly from the Guiana coast to northern Hispaniola sometime in the late 700s A.D., when Meillacan pottery first appears. They base their hypothesis on the presence of artifactual and other cultural traits shared by Meillacan-Macorís culture with, particularly, the Mabaruma phase of the Akawabi archaeological complex of the Guianas (Veloz Maggiolo, Ortega, and Caba Fuentes 1981:372–397; Evans and Meggers 1960). While the present authors are not personally convinced on archaeological grounds alone that such a migration was necessary to account for the Meillacan-Macorís peculiarities, the single anomalous form *baeza* raises serious questions concerning the overall input sources to Macorís culture, and we are convinced that the Veloz Maggiolo–Ortega–Caba Fuentes hypothesis is worthy of considerable further testing.

It must be pointed out that there is other evidence, discussed subsequently, which points to a non-Arawakan origin for the Macorís language, and we are consequently not, on the basis of the single known Macorís word *baeza*, postulating Macorís as an Arawakan tongue. Some Arawakan source, other than Taíno, however, did provide input to the language, but there were other more dominant non-Arawakan inputs as well.

THE CIBONEY TAÍNO LANGUAGE DATA

There is only one other non–Classic Taíno word used by the chroniclers. This is, not surprisingly, another word for 'gold,' and it is specifically attributed to the Lucayans. Las Casas says:

> He [a Ciguayo] calls gold *tuob* and does not understand the word *caona* as it is called in the major part of the island, nor *nozay*, as they call it on San Salvador and in the other islands. (Las Casas 1875:I:282)
> [*Llamaba al oro tuob y no entendía por caona, como le llamaban en la primera parte de la isla, ni por nozay como lo nombran en San Salvador y en las otras islas*]

He says the same thing later in the *Historia* (1875:I:434) and goes into greater detail in yet another passage:

> the Admiral commanded that [in the Lucayan Islands] they neither accept nor take anything except gold, which they call *nuçay;* although I do not think that the Christian Indians [i.e. of Hispaniola] would understand, since in the language of this island of Hispaniola (and all these islands use one language), where they call gold *caona*, the Indians wouldn't say *nuçay*. (Las Casas 1875:I:326)
> [*mandó el Almirante que no se les recibiese ni tomase alguna, porque supiesen,*

dizque, no buscar al Almirante (en las Islas Lucayas) sino oro, a quien ellos llaman nuçay; aunque yo creo que los cristianos no entendían, porque como todas estas islas hablasen una lengua, la desta Isla Esapñola donde llaman el oro caona, no debían decir los indios nuçay]

The Taíno word *caona* has cognates in all the other Northern Maipuran Arawakan languages—Island Carib *kaouánam,* for example. *Nozay* or *nuçay* has no etymology in either Arawakan or Cariban languages. It has a close parallel, however, in Modern Warao *naséi símo,* 'gold.' Warao is a language of isolated stock, perhaps ultimately Macro-Chibchan, of the Orinoco Delta in Venezuela and Guyana. *Naséi símo* consists of the morphemes *naséi* 'pebble' + *símo* 'yellow or reddish-colored' (Williams 1928:240, 246; 1929:201, 216, 222). The similarity between Warao *naséi* and what in Lucayan would phonetically be *nosái* is striking, and the meaning of the form, 'pebble,' quite appropriate.

As pointed out earlier, the speech of at least the central and northern Lucayan Islands seems to have been mutually intelligible with the speech of the Ciboney of the north-central coast of Cuba (Columbus in Fuson 1987:100, 103, 107, *et passim*). It is therefore reasonable to assume that the Lucayan word *nosái* is presumably a Ciboney Taíno word and implies some type of Waroid language contact for the Ciboney. This logic will be pursued further in the chapters on toponyms and on archaeological correlates of the language data.

We also know that the Cuban Ciboney dialect of Taíno, while mutually intelligible with the Hispaniolan dialects, had its own idiosyncratic use of various words and phrases (Las Casas 1875:I:315, 359, *et passim*). Other than *nosái,* however, which by association we are suggesting is a Lucayan Ciboney Taíno word, we have no lexical forms in the sources which are specifically labeled by Las Casas as Ciboney.

A CLASSIC TAÍNO ANOMALOUS FORM

To this data must be added the Classic Taíno word *duho,* 'ceremonial stool.' This particular lexical form, by rights, should not be found in Taíno, for as *duhu* it is the Warao word for 'sit, stool,' and there is no phonologically similar base in any Arawakan language with that meaning, nor can we convincingly derive *duho* from some other phonologically similar Arawakan form with the same meaning by rules of regular sound correspondence.

The general Arawakan, Northern Maipuran base for 'sit' is -*la,* as in Lokono *bálatin,* Goajiro *áikkalaa* (Taylor 1977:132, 135). While Classic Taíno had an *l* phoneme, it occurred only form-finally. Its realization after an unstressed vowel in form-medial position in other Northern Maipuran languages is usually reflected in Taíno as *n*—as in Lokono *kallípina* 'Carib,' Taíno *kaníba,* or

Lokono *búddali* 'griddle,' Taíno *burén*. When it occurs after a stressed vowel in other Northern Maipuran languages, as well as when it occurs form-initially, it is realized in Taíno as *y*—as in Lokono l*o*- 'person (specifically Indian),' Taíno y*u*-, or Lokono *máliaba* 'guava,' Taíno *wayaba*. A phonetic *h* in Taíno, on the other hand, is usually the reflex either of an *h* in other Maipuran languages or of an *r*—as in Lokono *baráa* 'sea,' Taíno *bahaua*, Lokono *-ári* 'tooth,' Taíno *-ahi*, Lokono h*ábba* 'basket,' Taíno h*aba*, Lokono *-náhalle* 'paddle,' Taíno *nahe*. That is, there is no regular correspondence between other Northern Maipuran languages and Taíno in which the phonetic *l* of the Northern Maipuran base *la*- 'sit' could become a phonetic *h* in Taíno. If the *-ho* segment of Taíno *duho* were derived from Northern Maipuran *-la*, the consonant should be either an *n* or a *y*. It is not. If, on the other hand, Taíno *duho* were derived from a Northern Maipuran base meaning 'sit' other than *la*-, then that base should contain either a phonetic *h* or a phonetic *y* as its primary consonant. There is no such base in Northern Maipuran. This rather lengthy discursion is important because it indicates that there is no possible Arawakan source for Taíno *duho,* and we are left with some Waroid language as its sole possible point of origin.

There is, however, one other Northern Maipuran language which does have a form similar to *duho*. This is Goajiro, which, as mentioned earlier, shares a number of interesting conservative Northern Maipuran traits with Taíno as well as several unique innovative traits. The Goajiro form for 'bench' is *tulú*. The *l-h* correspondence, while infrequent, does occur between Goajiro and other North Maipuran languages (Taylor 1977:43). The Goajiro form *tulú*, in other words, may also come from a Waroid *duhu* source. Like Taíno *duho*, Goajiro *tulú* has no convincing Arawakan etymology. The Goajiro people, however, have lived embedded in territory which is known from toponymic evidence to have been occupied by Waroid speakers for most of the last four millennia (Wilbert 1957).

Both Goajiro and Taíno are peripheral Northern Maipuran languages, off to one side geographically from the Río Negro-Orinoco heartland. It may be that the ancestors of both peoples were at one time in contact somewhere along the upper or middle course of the Orinoco and at that time borrowed the term *duhu* from their Waroid neighbors. Why such a borrowing? It may be that certain religious and sociopolitical concepts involving the *duho* were adapted from Waroid sources, bringing with them an associated Waroid vocabulary, for *duhos* were not the ordinary chairs of the Taíno, but, rather, stools of the aristocratic class alone. Were this the case, one would expect both a wider set of ceremonial words and a relatively enduring set of ceremonial customs to link the Warao, the Goajiro, and the Taíno. This is not, however, the case. An alternate possibility is that *duho* was borrowed by the Taíno *in* Hispaniola, after the ancestral Taíno had arrived and were in contact with the Archaic Age people

Table 2. Summary of Anomalous Greater Antillean Language Forms

Language	Form			Morphs	Parallels	Origin
	Spelling	Gloss	Phonetic			
Ciguayo	tuob	gold	twób	to- -w- -b(e)	E. Tol t('heavy(ness)') E. Tol -w- 'its' E. Tol -pe 'stone' W. Tol -be 'stone' Proto-Tol *pe 'stone' Proto-Pomo *-be, -bé 'stone' Proto-Yuman *-wi()(y) 'stone' Hokan Chontal -bik 'stone'	Tolan
	Quizquella	very mountainous	kʰiskʰeya	kʰis -kʰe- -ya	E. Tol kʰis 'hard rock' E. Tol reduplication E. Tol yo 'tree'	
Macorís	baeza	no	baésa	ba- -ésa	N Maipuran ma- 'negative' Paresis ba- 'negative' Gen'l Maipuran -Vti 'thing' Manao -ésa 'thing' Paresis -isa 'thing'	Eastern Maipuran (?)
Ciboney Taíno	nozay	gold	nosái	nosái	Warao naséi 'pebble' naséi simo 'gold'	Waroid
Classic Taíno	duho	stool	dúho	dúho	Warao dúhu 'sit, stool'	Waroid

of the island. As we shall see in the discussion of archaeological data in the next chapter, the Venezuelan-Guianan coastal origin of the Greater Antillean Archaic Age people indicates that they may, indeed, have been speakers of a Waroid language.

We have only the above lexical forms to go on in attempting to characterize Ciguayo. The Macorís and Ciboney Taíno lexical data are supplemented by additional toponymic data which is handled in the subsequent chapter on that topic. The lexical forms discussed in this chapter are summarized in Table 2. Their tentative linguistic analysis, obviously, cannot alone provide any final answers. We must look to other data—ethnohistorical, archaeological, and toponymic—for additional clarification.

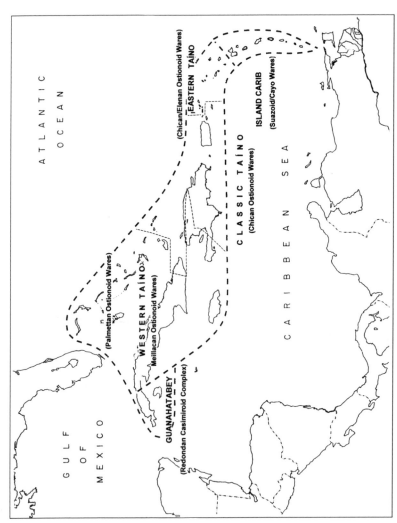

Fig. 5. Antillean Ethnic/Archaeological Units in 1492

4

The Primary Archaeological Correlates of Language Data from the Greater Antilles and Their Outliers

The available archaeological data from the Greater Antilles, the Lucayan Islands, and the Virgin Islands match the linguistic data discussed in the previous chapters remarkably well. As Rouse (1986, 1992), Kozłowski (1975), and Veloz Maggiolo (1976) have recently summarized, the earliest known human occupation of the Antilles is that defined by the Lithic Age complexes of Cuba and Hispaniola—called *Casimiroid* by Rouse, *Seboruco-Mordán* by Kozłowski, and *Mordanoid* by Veloz Maggiolo—with an approximate initiation date of 4,000 B.C. All the sites of this early lithic series are so closely related that they have been placed into a single subseries, the Casimiran, which expresses itself locally through the Seboruco site and people in Cuba, the Cabaret site and people in Haiti, and the Casimira and Barrera-Mordán sites and people in the Dominican Republic (Rouse 1992:13–15). Though initially thought to be limited to the two largest islands of the Greater Antilles, Gus Pantel has located a Casimiroid site in Puerto Rico at Cerillo, just across the Mona Passage from the eastern end of Hispaniola (Pantel 1988:70–75). There is no clear indication of further extension of the earlier Casimiroid peoples—approximately 4190–2165 B.C.—into Jamaica, the Greater Antillean Outliers (the Lucayan Islands and the Cayman Islands), or the Lesser Antilles.

Though an origin on the Colombian or Venezuelan coast has been suggested for the Casimiroid culture and people (Veloz Maggiolo and Ortega 1976), the most probable origin for these lithic complexes lies in Belize and Honduras at approximately 7500 B.C. (Coe 1957, Hahn 1960:268–280, MacNeish 1982:38–48, Rouse 1986:129–134, Rouse 1992:51–57). As we have seen, the sparse Ciguayo language data also support a Central American origin for this tradition.

A second migration into the Antilles, from the Guiana coast of South America with an ultimate origin not unlikely in Falcón State on the Waroid-speaking Venezuelan littoral, began at approximately 2000 B.C. (Allaire 1997a:21, Rouse 1992:69, Wilbert 1957). From the earliest traces of the artifactual inventory of these peoples at the Banwari Trace and Ortoire sites on Trinidad, the complex had reached that island by shortly before 5000 B.C. (Rouse 1992:62). This complex has been called *Ortoiroid,* after the Trinidadian type-site, and marks an Archaic Age complex of aceramic culture traits. We know from radiocarbon dates with a spread from 2150 B.C. to 190 A.D. (Rouse 1992:82)—at the Sugar Factory site on St. Kitts (2150 B.C.), the Jolly Beach site on Antigua (1775 B.C.), a site on Saba (1205 B.C.), from sites on Vieques (1060 B.C.–190 A.D.), at the Krum Bay and Estate Betty's Hope sites in the Virgin Islands (800–225 B.C.), and from the Coroso site in Puerto Rico (624 A.D.), as well as sites on St. Vincent—that Ortoiroid peoples and cultures had reached the edge of the Greater Antilles sometime before 1000 B.C., perhaps earlier (Figueredo 1976, 1987; Goodwin 1978; Gross 1976; Lundberg 1989, 1991; Rouse 1992:62; Rouse and Allaire 1979:114).

These Lesser Antillean Archaic cultures are difficult to characterize because of the small numbers of artifacts recovered, because there is so much variation from site to site, and because the artifactual inventory of most sites is not always typically Ortoiroid (Kozłowski 1980:71–74, Rouse 1986:132, Rouse 1992:62, Veloz Maggiolo and Ortega 1973). Most archaeologists working in the region attribute these diverse characteristics to a process of hybridization of Ortoiroid traits with traits from other sources, largely Casimiroid (Davis 1974:69–70, Veloz Maggiolo 1976), and Rouse (1986:106–107) reminds us to bear in mind that both transculturation and acculturation played as important a part in the development of Greater Antillean cultures as the physical migration of peoples. That there was either interaction between earlier Casimiroid peoples in the Lesser Antilles or borrowing of some lithic artifactual types and manufacturing techniques from Casimiroid peoples farther north in Puerto Rico seems clear from artifacts at the Jolly Beach site on Antigua and from sites on Vieques (Davis 1974, Lundberg 1989:165–169). Rouse (1992:68) refers to such cultures as "dual cultures," one part of the duality being Ortoiroid, the other Casimiroid. The artifact inventory from the Cayo Cofresí site on Puerto Rico's southern coast provides a particularly good example of such a dual, hybridized culture.

A direct Ortoiroid input to the cultures of Hispaniola and Cuba is also difficult to recognize, and many archaeologists consider the Ortoiroid peoples and tradition to have halted their movement through the Antilles in Puerto Rico, creating a frontier between themselves and the Casimiroid peoples on the two large islands to their west. This frontier is envisioned as being relatively lasting and stable from approximately 1000 to 400 B.C. (Rouse 1992:67–70). As Rouse (1992:67) points out, the data we presently have indicate that the direction of trait diffusion seems to have been "entirely from northwest to southeast—from, that is, the Casimiroid peoples."

On the other hand the majority of the Archaic cultures of both the Greater

Antilles—the *Redondan* in Cuba (with 24 radiocarbon dates spanning the period from 2050 B.C. to 1300 A.D.), the *Courian* in Hispaniola (with 29 radiocarbon dates from 2660 B.C. to 240 A.D.), and the *Corosan* in Puerto Rico—as well as Lesser Antillean sites with dates ranging from 2150 B.C. to 190 A.D., show both Ortoiroid artifactual traits, such as the presence of bone projectile points and barbs, shell celts, and edge-grinders, and Casimiroid traits, such as the presence of ground-stone artifacts (Rouse 1992:57–67). As Rouse (1992:67) points out, "the irregular distribution of types of flint, ground-stone, and shell tools is more difficult to explain." The Casimiroid contribution to the Courian and Redondan cultures of the Greater Antilles clearly dominates those complexes, while the Ortoiroid contribution is dominant in the Archaic cultures of the Lesser Antilles.

We are left, in short, with a number of variant hypotheses: either Ortoiroid interaction across the Mona Passage frontier between 1000 and 400 B.C. was a matter of transculturation and borrowing, or there was a physical movement of Ortoiroid people(s) across that frontier into the Greater Antilles (Rouse 1992:67–70). Archaeologists are divided in their opinion. Rouse (1992) favors transculturation as the dominant form of interaction; Veloz Maggiolo (1980) favors a more direct interaction. Whatever the actual situation, the end result was, for all the Antilles, Archaic cultures which were creolized, hybrid, or in at least some sense dual in nature.

Inasmuch as the Waroid peoples are known to have inhabited the north coast of South America from western Lake Maracaibo to the Guianas, particularly the Orinoco Delta, during the past three to four millennia, the origin and development of the Ortoiroid cultural tradition is usually associated with them (Wilbert 1957). If we find linguistic evidence for Waroid speakers on Hispaniola and Cuba, as we do, then we should be finding Ortoiroid sites, or at least sites with a strong Ortoiroid input. To date we have not found such sites, unless the later Casimiroid *Redondan* and *Courian* traditions of Cuba and Hispaniola respectively do indeed have trait elements attributable to an Ortoiroid source, as Veloz Maggiolo suggests with his use of the term *Hybridoid* to describe the later Casimiroid cultures of Hispaniola (Kozłowski 1975, Rouse 1992:57–61, Veloz Maggiolo and Ortega 1976).

Pervasive creolization, it should be pointed out, requires neither a large invasive population nor a lengthy time-span. The Norman conquest of England provides an apt comparison, taking a handful of newcomers and their descendants only two centuries—1066 to 1250—to turn Anglo-Saxon culture into Norman English culture and the Germanic Old English language into a thoroughly relexified and restructured Romanicized Middle English. We will have to wait for substantiating archaeological data before we will be able to say whether this kind of process took place between the Ortoiroid and Casimiroid peoples of the Greater Antilles. There seems, however, to have been a fairly rapid east to west spread of ideas and, one assumes, people through the Greater Antilles during the Archaic, for new tool-working techniques and artifactual types, particularly shell, are present in far western Cuba by 2050 B.C., to judge from radiocarbon dates for the Guayabo Blanco complex site of Residuario Fuenche in Pinar del Río province (Rouse and Allaire 1979:117). Later versions of the cultural complex, referred to as the Cayo Redondo complex, with greater emphasis on ground-stone artifact types, occur at Mogote de la Cueva, radiocarbon dated to 1300 A.D., and survived well into historical times as the Guanahatabey culture, as Diego Velázquez de Cuellar's 1514 report suggests.

The archaeological data, regardless of the variant views of the Greater Antillean Archaic, fit well both with the distribution of Waroid toponyms and with the occurrence of place-names containing the word "Macorís." Such data provide agreement with the suggestion that the language of the Greater Antillean Archaic Age peoples was non-Arawakan and Warao-related.

When the pre-Taíno Arawak of the pottery-making Cedrosan Saladoid tradition reached Puerto Rico and the eastern end of Hispaniola in what seems to have been a very rapid advance from locations somewhere in an area on the eastern Venezuelan coast to the Wonotobo Valley in Suriname, it confronted the Archaic peoples (Allaire 1997a, Haviser 1997, Watters 1997). This remarkably speedy migration took place during the period from approximately 400 B.C. (more conservatively, perhaps 200 B.C.) to the early years of the Christian era.

During the same time-period a related but differing pottery-making tradition, the Huecan Saladoid tradition, reached the same end-point—at least as far as Vieques and the eastern end of Puerto Rico (Chanlatte Baik, 1981, 1983; Rodríguez 1991). The origins of this pottery style may have been the Río Chico area of the central Venezuelan coast, for Huecan wares show a high degree of similarity to Río Guapo wares from that area (Rouse and Cruxent 1963:108–110, Rouse 1992: 88).

After halting at the Mona Passage and eastern Hispaniola frontier for approximately 400 years, the pre-Taíno peoples began to manufacture locally inspired ceramic wares of the Ostionoid tradition—Ostionan in western Puerto Rico and eastern Hispaniola and Elenan in eastern Puerto Rico and the Leeward Islands (Rouse 1986:134–143, 1992:90–96, 123–127). Between that time and approximately 800 A.D. the early Taíno were not only developing their own unique culture traits but were also absorbing traits from their Archaic Age neighbors as they gradually melded with them in their inexorable move westward. Part of this Archaic Age heritage may have been the word *duho* and at least some of the accompanying socio-religious traits later so diagnostic of Classic Taíno culture (Oliver 1997; Petitjean-Roget 1997a, 1997b; Rodríguez

1997; Stevens-Arroyo 1988). Ostionan traits had completely replaced Archaic Age traits in eastern and central Hispaniola by approximately 800 A.D. It seems clear from the archaeological record that by that date the Taíno had culturally absorbed the Archaic cultures of most of Hispaniola except in the far north-western regions, which became Macorís territory, where the inhabitants were still struggling against complete Taíno absorption at the time of Spanish arrival, and, of course, the still remaining Tolan Ciguayo enclave on the Samaná Peninsula in the far northeast of the island.

The Taíno so influenced the Macorís that they, too, had become pottery makers, of the new and distinctive Meillacan Ostionoid styles, blending Archaic Age art motifs with Taíno ceramic techniques. Just as Ostionan wares had made their way eastward from the Puerto Rican and Hispaniolan homeland to the Virgin Islands as Elenan wares (Rouse and Allaire 1979:116; Rouse 1992:95, Figueredo 1987:7), so Meillacan wares made their way westward from northern Hispaniola to eastern and central Cuba as Baní wares, to Jamaica as White Marl wares, and to the Lucayan Islands, first as Meillacan trade wares and then as local wares of the new Palmettan subseries of the Ostionoid ceramic series—Palmetto Ware, Abaco Redware, and Crooked Island Ware (Berman and Gnivecki 1991, 1995; Granberry and Winter 1995; Hoffman 1970:16–22; MacLaury 1970:41–42). Radiocarbon dates indicate that the basic Meillac style originated in Macorís territory sometime during the 700s A.D. (Veloz Maggiolo, Ortega, and Caba Fuentes 1981:397–399).

It is the constellation of culture traits found in Macorís territory, westward into Cuba and Jamaica, and northward into the Lucayan Islands, of which Meillacan ware is one, that archaeologists use to define what was initially called the Sub-Taíno Tradition, now more aptly referred to simply as the Western Taíno tradition (Lovén 1935:vi, Rouse 1992:7–8). It coincides nicely with ethnic Cuban Ciboney, Lucayan, and western Hispaniolan (Haitian) ethnohistoric descriptions. Just as Las Casas's ethnographic accounts indicate a way of life for the Macorís, Ciboney, and Lucayo that is different from that of the Hispaniolan Taíno, so the archaeological record indicates a significant difference in artifactual inventory. The archaeological data match the ethnographic data well, and, as we have seen, the suggested Ciboney dialect of Taíno was defined largely from the ethnographic base. It is in those areas that we postulate, on ethnographic and linguistic grounds, that the old, Waroid language neither survived, as in Macorís territory, nor was replaced, as in central and eastern Hispaniola, but, rather, was creolized with Taíno to become the Ciboney dialect of that language, in much the same manner that Old English creolized with Norman French to become Middle English.

Most archaeologists do see Western Taíno culture as the end result of a process of a mixture of various kinds between the cultures of the Archaic Age peoples of western Hispaniola, Cuba, and Jamaica and the Taíno culture. The traits atypical of Taíno culture are usually attributed to an ultimate Archaic Age source (Rouse 1992). Veloz Maggiolo, Ortega, and Caba Fuentes, however, feel that the full range of Western Taíno traits, particularly Meillacan ceramic decorative norms and, most notably, the use of *montículo y várzea* (river-bank mound) techniques of manioc cultivation, point to a non-Taíno yet Arawakan source, coming directly to Hispaniola from the Guianas sometime in the eighth century A.D. (Veloz Maggiolo, Ortega, and Caba Fuentes 1981:376–397). We have already commented on the provocative Macorís language form *baésa,* which, though clearly Arawakan, cannot have a Taíno or Eyeri source, but it is the senior author's feeling, admittedly nonempirical, that archaeological data alone are insufficient for postulating a full-blown migration from the Guianas to northern Hispaniola as a means of explaining the non-Taíno cultural peculiarities of Western Taíno culture. Much work, both archaeological and linguistic, is called for to clarify the problem.

The archaeological data do, in any case, define a Western Taíno cultural tradition, it does have its source in Macorís lands in the early 700s A.D., and it does spread to all Greater Antillean areas known to have been inhabited by the Ciboney or groups ethnohistorically identified as similar or identical with the Ciboney, such as the people of Cuba (Febles and Rives 1991, Guarch Delmonte 1973, Tabío and Rey 1979), and the Lucayans (Las Casas 1875:I:294) and the inhabitants of western Hispaniola (Las Casas 1875:III:463 *et passim;* V:243, 266). Such an expansion penetrated at least as far as San Salvador in the central Bahamas and Grand Turk in the Turks and Caicos by the late 700s or early 800s A.D. (Berman and Gnivecki 1991, 1995; Keegan and Carlson 1997). Such a rapid spread was undoubtedly facilitated by the widespread use of very large, very seaworthy sailing canoes (Bernáldez 1930:124; Major 1870:9–10; McKusick 1960, 1970; Watters 1997).

In approximately 1200 A.D. the Taíno of the Hispaniolan heartland began to produce a new style of ceramic wares, referred to as Chican Ostionoid. This, along with significant developments in socio-political and religious life, often referred to as a florescence (Hoffman 1980), is one of the diagnostic characteristics of the Classic Taíno way of life. Chican ware spread from Hispaniola eastward into Puerto Rico and the Leeward Islands as far south as Saba (Morse 1997:45) and westward into Haiti and, just before the arrival of the Spanish, into Cuba and the southern Lucayan Islands (see for the latter, De Booy 1912; Sullivan 1980, 1981).

That the expansion of Chican culture was still ongoing at the time of the Spanish arrival is clear not only from Las Casas's statements that the Taíno had begun to settle Cuba only 50 years earlier (Las Casas 1875:III:463), but from the archaeological record as well. It would seem fairly certain that Taíno expansion into western Hispaniola, present-day Haiti, was also in process and had not been initiated much before 1300. Marién Kingdom (see Figure 2), for example, was certainly still part of a frontier between the creolized Ciboney and the Taíno, though the chroniclers never apply the term "Ciboney" to the inhabitants of the western part of the island. We find, for example, sites such as Bois de Charrité near Cap Haïtien in northern Haiti, radiocarbon dated to 1250–1350 A.D., with only Meillacan wares (Ortega and Guerrero 1982:29–53); sites such as Bois Neuf in west-central Haiti from the same period in which Meillacan and Chican wares occur in the same strata (Rainey and Ortiz Aguilú 1983); and sites such as En Bas Saline, probably the location of Columbus's first, abortive settlement in the New World, La Navidad, radiocarbon dated to 1270–1350, in which only Chican wares occur (Deagan 1987:345). En Bas Saline is particularly important since it was probably the chief town of Guacanagarí, the Taíno ruler of Marién province and kingdom at the time of Columbus's arrival.

The archaeological data seem to be telling us that there were contemporary settlements in western Hispaniola in which only makers and users of Meillacan ware lived (Bois de Charrité), others in which only makers and users of Chican wares lived (En Base Saline), and yet others in which the makers and users of both pottery styles lived side by side (Bois Neuf). We would suggest, as Rouse (1986:1243) has for the La Hueca and Sorcé wares of Vieques, that we are perhaps dealing with an underlying social dichotomy, in this instance between a Taíno elite and the Hispaniolan underclass, reflected artifactually in the expected use by each group of its own dominant artifactual types and styles, perhaps, to use Rouse's analogy, something akin to the difference between chinaware use by the more affluent and stoneware use—nowadays Melamac!—by the less affluent in European and Euro-American cultures. In communities such as Bois de Charrité, inhabited only by the less privileged, the creolized Hispaniolan Macorís whom we are calling Hispaniolan Ciboney, we find only "stoneware" (Meillacan wares); in communities such as En Bas Saline, inhabited only by the politically dominant newcomers, the Taíno, we find only "chinaware" (Chican wares); and in communities such as Bois Neuf, inhabited by both populations, we find both wares, distributed unevenly in different areas of the site though in the same strata.

We need, generally, the excavation of many more Haitian sites, much more controlled excavation, and better distributional studies both within single sites as well as from site-to-site before we can be sure if we are dealing with this kind of situation. The implication, at least, is that western Hispaniola had not yet been fully Taínoized by the time of Spanish arrival, that outside of the Taíno towns it was still essentially "Ciboney."

There are no indications that the Lucayan periphery was ever settled by Lithic Age Casimiroid peoples. There are, however, some indications that first human settlement may have taken place at some time between 2000 B.C. and the early centuries of the Christian Era by bearers of aceramic Archaic Redondan and/or Courian Casimiroid culture, presumably entering the islands from the northeastern coast of Cuba and/or the northern coast of Hispaniola.

The late Herbert W. Krieger of the U.S. National Museum reported in 1937 that he had located what he called Ciboney-like (i.e., Guanahatabey) aceramic sites in the Berry Islands, to the immediate northwest of New Providence, as well as on Andros Island (Krieger 1937:98). He neither locates them nor discusses the artifactual materials recovered, however, nor would he allow the senior author to examine the artifacts when requested during the late 1940s. He adds that the sites were shell middens identical in nature to those at Île-à-Vache off the southern coast of Haiti (see Rouse 1947, 1982; Moore 1982) and on the Samaná Peninsula in the Dominican Republic (Krieger 1929). The materials from the Haitian and Dominican sites are demonstrably Courian Casimiroid in nature, though we unfortunately have no radiocarbon dates for the sites themselves. Because of the lack of follow-up on the initial 1937 report, Krieger's statement has generally been taken as erroneous, though Krieger was usually a capable and reliable professional, and his statements are certainly worthy of further investigation.

Two non-ceramic sites with characteristics similar to those classified by Osgood (1942) as "Ciboney" (i.e. Guanahatabey) have, however, been located in the Bahamas: one, the South Victoria Beach site on Paradise Island, off New Providence, the other, the Gold Rock Creek site, on the south coast of Grand Bahama (see Bahamas Archaeological Team 1984 for a summary report on the South Victoria Beach site). Both sites are located in sheltered coves, are ring-shaped shell middens, and contain *Strombus* (conch) awl-like points which are quite distinctive, not present in ceramic-bearing Lucayan sites, and similar to those reported by Osgood (1942) for Redondan sites in Cuba. The South Victoria Beach site, now unfortunately destroyed by the Atlantis development, has been radiocarbon dated to 1100–1226 A.D. (820 +/− 60 B.P., Beta Labs #27220), perhaps indicating a late Guanahatabey-like settlement from Cuba in the Lucayan archipelago.

The central and southern Lucayan Islands were certainly settled by Ostionan peoples, probably from northeastern Cuba, around 600 A.D. (Berman and Gnivecki 1991) and by later Meillacan peoples from both Cuba and Hispaniola by the early 800s (Rouse 1992). The latter migration of what we have called Ciboney Taíno speakers is supported by the toponyms *Bimini* and *Lucayoneque*, which are discussed in Chapter 7. Work by Bill Keegan and Betsy Carlson at the Coralie Site on Grand Turk (Keegan and Carlson 1997) and accompanying radiocarbon dates make it clear that the Turks and Caicos had been settled sometime during the 700s A.D. Such settlement may have come from the northern coast of Haiti or the Dominican Republic, but at least one researcher, noting the close similarities between Lucayan Palmettan wares and Virgin Islands Magen's Bay wares, has suggested a possible origin in the Virgin Islands or Puerto Rico (Hoffman 1970:44, 1974).

Work by Shaun Sullivan in the Caicos Islands indicates that Classic Taíno speakers, probably from the north coast of Hispaniola, entered the Lucayan Islands about 1200 A.D., settling the Turks and Caicos and bringing with them both Hispaniola-produced Chican ceramic wares and the concepts of Chican ceramic decorative motifs, which spread north into at least the central islands of the Bahamas (Sullivan 1980, 1981; Granberry and Winter 1995). Such a late Classic Taíno presence in the Lucayan Islands is substantiated by the known fact that the ruler of powerful Maguana kingdom in Hispaniola, Caonabó, was a native Lucayan (Las Casas 1875:V:482).

Archaeological and ethnolinguistic data, then, indicate that the Ciguayo of 1492 were the last cultural, or at least linguistic, descendants of a Tolan Casimiroid people whose origins lie in Belize-Honduras. We need to know more about Ciguayo material culture from controlled excavation in the areas in which they are known to have survived—the Samaná Peninsula.

Archaic cultures, originating in the Waroid-speaking littoral of northern South America, seem gradually to have succumbed to Taíno pressure from about 400 A.D. onward. In Puerto Rico and eastern and central Hispaniola they were completely replaced or absorbed by the late 700s and early 800s, and those regions became the heartland of Classic Taíno culture. The spread of early Taíno culture, as evidenced by the distribution of Ostionan ceramic wares, was far-reaching, but beyond central Hispaniola it seems to have produced only a veneer of Taínoization, as among the Upper and Lower Macorís, who still spoke their own language and had their own rulers. The same situation, with somewhat more Taínoization in which a creolized amalgam, part Taíno, part Archaic Age Macorís, which we came to know as the Ciboney, was produced. Archaic traditions survived, seemingly intact, only with the Guanahatabey people in far western Cuba. Their distance from the center of Taíno and later Spanish power seems to have insured their survival until at least the 1600s, perhaps beyond, if local Cuban oral traditions of remnant Indian populations in the late 1800s or even the early 1900s are true.

Meillacan wares are the diagnostic archaeological trait of the creolized cultures of the Greater Antilles and the Lucayan periphery, and they reflect the *Western Taíno* tradition. Chican wares are the diagnostic archaeological trait of heartland *Classic Taíno* culture and its colonial outposts, which were yet spreading further and further afield at the time the Spanish arrived (see Figure 6).

5
Languages of the Greater Antilles
A Working Hypothesis

To summarize the data of the previous chapters, the ethnohistoric record indicates that there were five different speech communities in the Greater Antilles at the time of Spanish intervention: *Classic Taíno, Ciboney Taíno, Macorís* in two dialects, *Ciguayo,* and *Guanahatabey.* The first two were dialects of a single Northern Maipuran Arawakan language, known simply as *Taíno.*

Ciguayo, a moribund language spoken only in the Samaná Peninsula region of Hispaniola in 1492 and extinct very shortly thereafter, has its closest parallels with the Honduran Tolan languages. Glottochronological data would suggest the separation of ancestral Ciguayo from the Tolan mainstream sometime before 3000 B.C. The position of the surviving speakers on Hispaniola implies that the Ciguayo were a remnant population of a once larger and more widespread group, forced into its 1492 geographical cul-de-sac by pressure from a later more dominant group entering the region from the south and east and pushing northward and westward through the Greater Antilles.

The shadowy Guanahatabey of far western Cuba fit the same geographical pattern, and, to judge from toponymic evidence, were possibly a remnant Waroid population forced into its geographical location by the movement of a more dominant people from the east.

All of the Greater Antillean language groups except Ciguayo show influence from a Waroid language. These parallels are lexical in Classic Taíno (*duho*) and Ciboney Taíno (*nosái*) (see Table 2), toponymic in both Macorís and Guanahatabey (see Table 4).

In addition, both north Hispaniolan Macorís and Lucayan Ciboney Taíno show lexical influence from some non-Taíno, non-Eyeri Maipuran Arawakan language in the forms *baésa* (Hispaniolan Macorís) and *Bímini* and *Lukayunéke* (Lucayan Ciboney Taíno).

Though the data are meager, it would seem both possible and desirable to postulate the following testable hypothesis:

(A) At some time prior to 3000 B.C. a Tolan-speaking people from the Belize-Honduras coastal region discovered and settled the then uninhabited Greater Antilles. Language data indicate their presence on, but do not necessarily limit their presence to, Hispaniola. Archaeological data indicate their presence in Cuba, Hispaniola, and Puerto Rico, with a probable presence in the Leeward Islands of the northern Lesser Antilles.

(B) At some time around 1000 B.C., a Waroid-speaking people from the northern South American coast was present in the Greater Antilles. Language data indicate its presence in, but not necessarily limited to, both Hispaniola and Cuba. Because of the Venezuelan affinities of Waroid speech, the hypothesis postulates a movement from that source to the Greater Antilles through the natural land bridge of the Lesser Antilles. Archaeological data indicates the presence of Archaic Age people in the Leeward Islands and the Greater Antilles, but not the Windward Islands, at this time period.

(C) The peripheral position of Ciguayo in 1492 may indicate that the newer Waroid population, while perhaps mixing with the older Tolan population, also forced at least some of the earlier Tolan speakers into less hospitable regions of the Greater Antilles.

(D) Toponymic evidence indicates that the Waroid language replaced the Tolan language throughout Hispaniola and Cuba except in the area occupied by the ethnohistoric Ciguayo.

(E) Around 1 A.D., from glottochronological data—around 200–400 A.D. from archaeological radiocarbon data—the Cedrosan Saladoid people, speaking a Northern Maipuran Arawakan language ancestral to Classic Taíno, began to move from the Guianas into the Lesser Antilles and on into the Greater Antilles.

(F) The Taíno language gradually replaced the Waroid language in Puerto Rico and in eastern and central Hispaniola. In western Hispaniola and Cuba it blended with the Waroid language to form a creolized idiom identified as the Ciboney dialect of Taíno. This dialect was largely Taíno in grammar and lexicon, but it seems to have retained some Waroid vocabulary. The creolization process accomplished itself during the period between 400 and 900 A.D., accompanying the western expansion of Ostionan and early Meillacan ceramic wares. Both people and their accompanying Ciboney Taíno dialect and Meillacan artifactual traits spread to the Lucayan islands toward the middle of this period (Berman and Gnivecki 1991, 1995).

(G) From toponymic and ethnohistoric evidence the Waroid language seems to have survived only in far western Cuba (the Guanahatabey) and in north coastal Hispaniola (Upper and Lower Macorís).

(H) Classic Taíno became a *lingua franca* for all the Greater Antilles except the Guanahatabey region of Cuba, which, from archaeological evidence, the

Taíno never penetrated. It also spread to the Turks and Caicos around 1200 A.D. with the migrations of the Classic Taíno–speaking people to those islands. This is evidenced by the presence of Chican ceramic wares in sites in that region and by historical tradition. About 1450 Classic Taíno also spread across Cabo Maisí from the northwestern peninsula of Haiti to what is now Oriente Province in far eastern Cuba. The latter migration was hastened and intensified by the arrival of the Spanish in 1492.

The testing of such a hypothesis will necessitate considerably more archaeological and linguistic research. A very important analytical dimension which might and should be added—not addressed to date by Antillean specialists—would be the gathering of serological and DNA evidence from both the living populations of the Greater Antilles and from pre-European skeletal remains. Both sources of hitherto ignored data are readily available to the qualified analyst.

6

The Languages of the Lesser Antilles and Their Archaeological Correlates

We have commented earlier that the identification and definition of Lesser Antillean aboriginal languages presents fewer problems than the identification and definition of the aboriginal languages of the Greater Antilles. While this is certainly the case, the difficulties of identifying and defining Lesser Antillean languages are far from fully resolved. We are, however, extremely fortunate in having copious language data on Eyeri-Kalíphuna, the primary language of the Lesser Antilles during proto-historic and historic times, for, unlike Taíno, which was no longer a viable spoken tongue by the mid- to late 1500s, Eyeri-Kalíphuna—called *Karifuna* by the remaining Native Americans on Dominica and *Garífuna* by its users in Central America—is still spoken by a large population in Belize, Guatemala, and Honduras, descendants of those forcibly removed there by the British in April of 1797.

It is also the case that although we still have much to learn about the original peopling of the Lesser Antilles, as well as about subsequent migrations to those islands, the general outline of archaeological sequences is relatively clear, and the task of correlating language data and archaeological data is less fraught with problems than in the Greater Antilles.

THE LITHIC AND ARCHAIC PERIODS

To date no sites comparable in age or artifactual content to the early period Casimiroid lithic sites of Cuba, Hispaniola, and Puerto Rico have been found in the Lesser Antilles. The earliest human habitation sites in the Lesser Antilles are, rather, Archaic Age sites containing non-Casimiroid, Ortoiroid, or at least Ortoiroid-like assemblages of ground-stone axes and pestles and copious tools of shell and bone (Allaire 1997a:21). These date from 2000 B.C. and later. These peoples and cultures had reached the edge of the Greater Antilles sometime before 1000 B.C., perhaps earlier (Figueredo 1976, 1987; Goodwin 1978; Gross

1976; Lundberg 1989, 1991; Rouse 1992:62; Rouse and Allaire 1979:114). All but a few such sites are located not in the southern, Windward Islands, as might be expected, but in the more northerly Leeward Islands—the Sugar Factory site on St. Kitts (2150 B.C.), the Jolly Beach site on Antigua (1775 B.C.), a site on Saba (1205 B.C.), a number of sites on Vieques (1060 B.C.–190 A.D.), the Krum Bay and Estate Betty's Hope sites in the Virgin Islands (800–225 B.C.), and the Coroso site in Puerto Rico (624 A.D.) (Allaire 1997a:21, Rouse 1992:62–67). The only sites located in the Windward Islands with comparable artifactual assemblages are the Buckamint site on St. Vincent and the two Boutbois sites on Martinique (Allaire and Mattioni 1983; Rouse 1992:53, 62–65). We do not, however, have secure dates for any of these three Windward Islands Archaic sites.

Given the general paucity of sites in the Windward Islands, Allaire (1997a: 21–22) has suggested the possibility that the non-Casimiroid Archaic Age assemblages found in Puerto Rico, on Vieques, in the Virgin Islands, and on Antigua, St. Kitts, and Saba may have developed locally in the Greater Antilles, their use gradually spreading south into the Leeward Islands, rather than originating on Trinidad and moving northwards—that the Greater Antillean and, by extension, Leeward Island sites may not, in other words, be Ortoiroid in the sense traditionally used in Caribbean archaeology (defined in Chapter 4). The fact, however, that the primary artifactual and site-location similarities between the Greater and Lesser Antillean aceramic Archaic Age sites lie with the Banwari Trace, Ortoire and related sites complex in Trinidad at the appropriate time level and that the latter assemblages are clearly related to Mainland sites from the Orinoco Delta region as far west along the Venezuelan littoral as Falcón State, whose western border fronts on Lake Maracaibo, would seem to contradict a local in-situ development of this tradition in the Greater Antilles. Ortoiroid sites on the Mainland and Trinidad span the time period from about 5250 to 450 B.C. (Rouse 1992:62; Rouse and Allaire 1979:108–109). There is additionally no other known cultural tradition which has the diagnostic characteristics of the Antillean sites in question, nor is there anything in the known prehistory of the Greater Antillean Casimiroid tradition which would point toward the innovations appearing in Archaic Age sites traditionally referred to as Ortoiroid.

Inasmuch as the Ortoiroid peoples were most likely speakers of a language ancestral to modern Warao (Wilbert 1957), as we have discussed and referenced in earlier chapters with both lexical and toponymic data from the Greater Antilles, it would seem difficult to explain the presence of a language of that stock in the Greater Antilles without a migration through the Lesser Antilles. It is of some interest to note in this same regard that quartz crystals, of unknown use, are found in Ortoiroid sites in Trinidad, and that such crystals are still in use as charms by the present-day Warao people of the Orinoco Delta (Lund-

berg 1991). While the source of the quartz may well have been the Greater Antilles, traded southward, it may equally as well have had a Mainland source,
traded northward from the ancestral Warao to their Pre-Columbian kinsmen
in Trinidad.

While so stating may be treading on very soggy ground until we have more
archaeological data, on the basis of both the Lesser Antillean archaeological
data we do have and Greater Antillean Waroid language data, it may be postulated that the Greater Antillean Ortoiroid peoples were the front-runners of a
general Ortoiroid movement into the Antilles from approximately 2000 B.C. to
approximately 500–600 B.C. The data gap in the Windward Islands still remains unexplained, as Allaire has pointed out, but this may as easily be a reflection of the fact that little in the way of concentrated modern archaeological
excavation, with accompanying radiocarbon dating, has been done on Guadeloupe, Dominica, Martinique, St. Lucia, and St. Vincent (see Delpuech 2001:21–
25). Only Grenada has seen a relatively thorough, but now somewhat outdated,
coverage (Bullen 1964). Because of the relatively small size of all of the islands
in the Lesser Antilles, it has additionally been suggested that Ortoiroid settlements there were likely small, transient, and intermittent (Keegan 1985:51–53;
Watters 1980:297). Archaeological data, particularly site frequency, location,
and size, would suggest that this hypothesis has merit and is well worth con-
sideration.

There are, nonetheless, still problems remaining, for, as pointed out in
Chapter 4, Lesser Antillean Archaic cultures are difficult to characterize because of the small numbers of artifacts recovered, because there is so much
variation from site to site, and because the artifactual inventory of most sites
is not always typically Ortoiroid (Kozłowski 1980:71–74; Rouse 1986:132; Rouse
1992:62; Veloz Maggiolo and Ortega 1973). Most archaeologists working in
the region attribute these diverse characteristics to a process of hybridization
of Ortoiroid traits with Casimiroid traits (Davis 1974:69–70; Veloz Maggiolo
1976). That there was either interaction with Casimiroid peoples on the edge
of the Lesser Antilles or borrowing of some lithic artifactual types and manufacturing techniques from Casimiroid peoples farther north in Puerto Rico
seems clear from artifacts at the Jolly Beach site on Antigua and from sites on
Vieques (Davis 1974; Lundberg 1989:165–169). Rouse (1992:68) refers to such
cultures as "dual cultures," one part of the duality being Ortoiroid, the other
Casimiroid.

In short, the nature and origins of earliest human settlement in the Lesser
Antilles still awaits further clarification, but the present consensus is that first
settlements were sporadic camps and transient communities established by
probably Waroid-speaking Ortoiroid people(s) from Trinidad whose cultural
origins lay further to the west along the Venezuelan coast; that they did not

remain long in one settlement; and that they had a preference for the less mountainous islands of the archipelago. As these settlers reached the Leeward Islands and Puerto Rico, they seem to have made contact with Casimiroid peoples and incorporated some modified Casimiroid artifactual modes into their otherwise Ortoiroid artifactual styles. This is what the data seem to be telling us, but for the present such an assessment is an hypothesis rather than an established theory.

THE EARLY CERAMIC PERIOD

At approximately 400–500 B.C. a new people, the ceramic-making, agricultural Cedrosan Saladoid people, appear on the scene. The nature of their culture and origins, unlike those of the Archaic Age peoples, is clear and unequivocal. Their origins lie in the Ronquinian Saladoid culture of Venezuela, whose settlements occur from the confluence of the Río Apuré and Orinoco Rivers in mid-central Venezuela and continue northeastward all along the course of the Orinoco some 400 miles to the river's delta on the Atlantic (Rouse 1992:75). Ronquinian sites have been radiocarbon dated to 2140 B.C. for the La Gruta site to approximately 620 B.C. for other sites (Rouse and Allaire 1979:99). In the Orinoco Delta, on the adjacent coastal region of eastern Venezuela, and on the island of Trinidad, the Ronquinian culture gradually developed into the Cedrosan Saladoid by 1000 B.C., defined by its type-site at Cedros on Trinidad (Rouse 1992:75).

The Cedrosan people, for reasons quite unknown, began to establish settlements northward into the Antilles around 500 B.C.—the Hope Estate site on St. Martin yields a radiocarbon date of 560 B.C., the earliest currently dated Cedrosan site in the Antilles (Haviser 1997:61). From the most recent study of settlement patterns in the Lesser Antilles and Puerto Rico during the Cedrosan Saladoid period (Haviser 1997), it is very evident that the movement of settlers was rapid, for the Fond Brulé site on Martinique has yielded a radiocarbon date of 530 B.C., the Trant's site on Montserrat a date of 480 B.C., and the Tecla site on Puerto Rico a date of 430 B.C. These earliest dates, except for the Fond Brulé site on Martinique, are concentrated in the Leeward Islands rather than in the Windwards, and we are faced with something like the Leeward-Windward time-gap we have for the Archaic Age. The earliest Windward Island Cedrosan dates are 36 A.D. for Grenada, 160 A.D. for St. Vincent, 490 A.D. for St. Lucia, and 50 A.D. for Guadeloupe. Just as it is not presently possible to explain the Archaic Age gap conclusively, so a final explanation cannot yet be given for the Cedrosan gap. In this instance, though, since we are certain that the origin of the Antillean Saladoid peoples was in Trinidad and the adjacent South American mainland, the apparent problem is probably not a problem at all, but again a reflection of our currently imperfect knowledge of the archaeology of Grenada, St. Vincent, St. Lucia, Dominica, Martinique, and Guadeloupe (see again Delpuech 2001:21).

We of course unfortunately have no language information from the Lesser Antilles, not even toponyms, at the Cedrosan Saladoid time level. Any statements about the language or languages spoken by the Cedrosan people(s) of the Antilles, both Greater and Lesser, must be made on the basis of inference. The inferences which we are able to make, however, are founded on quite solid data.

We are, for example, certain that the Saladoid cultures all had their origins in Arawakan-speaking areas of Amazonian Venezuela and the Guianas. Arawakan languages are recorded for these regions from the time of earliest European settlement to the present (Matteson 1972; Noble 1965; Taylor 1977). It is also known that the language we call Taíno was a member of the Maipuran branch of the Arawakan language family (Matteson 1972; Noble 1965; Taylor 1977 among others). This is the largest and most widespread branch of the Arawakan language family, with speakers in pre-Columbian times from the northern Bahamas to the Gran Chaco of Bolivia and from the Atlantic shores of the Guianas to the Lake Maracaibo region of western Venezuela and the foothills of the Peruvian Andes. There is considerable variation among these languages, but they are grouped together because they all share certain characteristics of sound, grammar, lexical formation, and lexical roots which are not present in the other Arawakan tongues. Maipuran itself can be subdivided into Northern, Eastern, and Southern language groups, the members of each of which, again, resemble one another in sound, grammar, and lexicon more than they do members of the other groups. The Northern languages are spoken all along the northern coast of South America from Lake Maracaibo in the west to the Atlantic in the east and as far inland as the confluence of the Río Negro and the Amazon, including the entire Orinoco Basin and the Guianas. Eastern Maipuran languages, such as Palicur and Marawan, are spoken on the Atlantic coast just north of the mouth of the Amazon, while other Eastern languages, such as Mehinacú and Waurá, are spoken in south central Brazil. The Southern Maipuran languages, such as Chané, Terreno, and Bauré, are spoken far to the south of the other Maipuran languages, in southwest Brazil and Bolivia (Migliazza 1985:22–23).

On the basis of lexical comparisons, Classic Taíno, as discussed in Chapters 2, 9, and 10, can be identified not only as a Maipuran language, but specifically as a Northern Maipuran language, for the bulk of its sound, grammatical, and lexical system shows closest similarities to those languages (Loukotka 1968:126–149; Matteson 1972:160–242).

Within Northern Maipuran it is also possible to distinguish a Northeast subgroup of languages and a Northwest subgroup. The major Northwest Maipuran languages are Goajiro, spoken to the west of Lake Maracaibo, Caquetío, now extinct, but formerly spoken along the coast in the Caracas and Isla Margarita region as well as on Aruba, Bonaire, and Curaçao, and Achagua and Piapoco, spoken further to the south in west-central Venezuela and the Upper Orinoco. The major Northeast Maipuran language still spoken today is the Arawak language proper, usually referred to by the native name Lokono. Speakers have been traditionally concentrated in the Guianas and Suriname from earliest known historic times to the present.

The greatest number of sound, grammatical, and lexical similarities between Classic Taíno and any of the Northern Maipuran languages occurs between Taíno and the Northwest Maipuran languages—Goajiro, Achagua, and Piapoco (Loukotka 1968:126–149; Matteson 1972:160–242; Noble 1965; Taylor 1977). One must recall, however, that we are comparing phonologically reconstructed fifteenth-century Taíno morphemes and lexical forms with forms from twentieth-century Northern Maipuran languages—a 500-year time-gap. One does not, therefore, expect data identities, but looks, rather, for regular recurring correspondences in sound and grammar. These are important, and they do occur, as indicated by the data in Chapters 9 and 10. Taíno, therefore, seems most logically assignable to the Northwest Maipuran language group, at a time when the language ancestral to the modern Northwest languages, Proto-Northwest Maipuran, had probably not yet differentiated into separate languages. Thus Classic Taíno and Early Goajiro, Early Caquetío, Early Achagua, and Early Piapoco were probably still but dialects of a single language, differing from one another in degree of mutual intelligibility to various degrees from slight to considerable depending upon the distance in time and space of their geographical separation. This would account for the shared features of Taíno and Goajiro discussed in Chapter 3.

Using Isidore Dyen's well-known model for language homeland reconstruction (Dyen 1956), the Northwest Maipuran homeland would have been somewhere in the area from south of Lake Maracaibo on the west and the confluence of the Río Apuré and the Orinoco on the east. This, the archaeological evidence suggests, is also the probable homeland of the Ronquinian Saladoid artifactual complex. In brief, the two models match, and it is therefore not at all out of the question to suggest that the Ronquinian people were speakers of one or more dialects of a Proto-Northwest Maipuran Arawak language and that they carried this language with them over the generations down the Orinoco to its delta and then northward into the Antilles. The time of their migration downriver to the delta seems to have spanned some 1,000 years, from approximately 2000 B.C. to 1000 B.C. (Roosevelt 1980:193–196; Rouse 1992:75), more than ample time to account for the language differences separating the dialects of Proto-Northwest Maipuran which were to become Goajiro, Achagua, and Piapoco both from each other and from that Proto-Northwestern Maipuran dialect which by then had become what was later to be called Taíno.

It is, then, hypothesized on the basis of this data-based series of inferences that the language of the Cedrosan Saladoid people, the language they brought with them to the Antilles about the year 500 B.C., was an early form of Taíno. This would have become the language of both the Lesser and Greater Antilles for a thousand years from that time until around 500 A.D.

THE LATE CERAMIC PERIODS

At about 500 A.D. a new element is added to the Cedrosan Saladoid ceramic inventory, namely the introduction of fresh, bold, innovative decorative techniques which derive from the Barrancoid tradition of the Orinoco Delta region of Venezuela. Rouse (1992:85) describes this change as Saladoid with Barrancoid influences, but Allaire (1997a:25) suggests that it might better be characterized as Barrancoid of Saladoid tradition, emphasizing the fact that although other than ceramically the old Cedrosan Saladoid culture assemblage seems to have remained intact and essentially unchanged, at the same time the ceramic wares of at least the Windward Islands became, in fact, pure Barrancoid, rather than Cedrosan with some Barrancoid influence.

The Barrancoid ceramic infusion affected all of the Windward Islands and, after 500 A.D., spread rapidly from Trinidad and Grenada northwards through Guadeloupe (Allaire 1997a:24–25; Rouse 1992:77, 85, 127). There is no evidence, however, that it penetrated the Leeward Islands or further north into the Greater Antilles (Rouse 1992:127), though Allaire (1997a:25) notes that Barrancoid influences on ceramic styles are noticeable at the Sorcé site on Vieques and at sites in the Virgin Islands that date to this period.

What seems increasingly obvious is that the Barrancoidization, if we may call it that, of the Windward Islands Cedrosan Saladoids was more than just a borrowing of ceramic design motifs and manufacturing techniques. Rouse, for example, notes the presence at the Sorcé and Punta Candelero sites on Vieques and the adjacent eastern coast of Puerto Rico of bird-head pendants of exotic stone, intricately and beautifully carved in the distinctive Barrancoid style (Rouse 1992:87). He adds that Linda Robinson communicated to him that similar pendants have been recovered from the Prosperity site on St. Croix, and José Oliver indicated that such pendants occurred in Barrancoid sites all along the lower Orinoco. That the Barrancoid people were an energetic and vigorous people is well indicated by their expansion from their origin-point in the eastern middle Orinoco Valley during the first millennium B.C. downstream to the river's delta and, by 500 A.D., their domination of the island of Trinidad (Rouse 1992:77; Allaire 1997a:25). They became the major trading society of the entire Orinoco region, as indicated by the wide geographical spread in which Barrancoid artifacts are found and in which Barrancoid artifactual influence is evident.

It thus seems more than likely that the presence of Barrancoid-inspired ceramics in the late Cedrosan Saladoid of the Windwards may have been as much or more the result of physical entrepreneurial population expansion northward from Trinidad as it was the borrowing of ceramic motifs by the Cedrosan people. That Barrancoid wares do not occur in the Leewards or further north adds fuel to the suggestion that the Barrancoid traders did not venture as permanent settlers further north than Guadeloupe.

Within a short time, during the late 500s to the mid-600s A.D., the Barrancoid-inspired late Cedrosan Saladoid wares of the Windward Islands had developed into a local style referred to as Troumassoid after the type site on St. Lucia. Troumassoid wares are found only in Barbados and on Grenada, St. Vincent, St. Lucia, Martinique, Dominica, and Guadeloupe—they do not extend northward into the Leeward Islands. In the Leewards, however, the Marmorean wares of Antigua and the Magens Bay wares of the Virgin Islands, though most closely allied in origin to the ceramics of Puerto Rico and Hispaniola, reflect clear Troumassoid influence, continuing the extension of Barrancoid influence to those islands a century and more earlier (Rouse 1992:127–129; Allaire 1997a:25–26).

It seems clear that the Cedrosan Saladoid peoples of the Windward Islands were joined by a Barrancoid population around 500 A.D.—in what numbers we do not and probably never will know, though the suspicion is that either the numbers must have been significant or the new population became politically and economically dominant regardless of its size. The Barrancoid influences are simply too great and too specific to have been the result of transculturative trait-borrowing by the Cedrosans, and, if the latter were the case, we are left with no explanation of the abrupt break in artifactual styles between Guadeloupe and the Leeward Islands. Whatever the case, it seems certain that the Windward Islands had a new or highly altered population by 500 A.D.

Because of the eastern, middle Orinoco origin of the Barrancoid tradition as well as its ultimate concentration in the Orinoco Delta region (Rouse 1992:77), it is unlikely that the Barrancoid people were speakers of a Northwest Maipuran language. It is much more likely that they spoke a Northeast Maipuran language, closely related to modern-day Lokono and the other Arawakan languages of the Guianas. Thus, if the Barrancoid trader-settlers of the Windwards became the dominant population of those islands following 500 A.D., their form of speech would either have replaced or strongly influenced the Taíno spoken on those islands during Cedrosan times. This new idiom would have become the language of the Windward Islands but not, to judge from archaeological evidence, of the Leewards.

We of course have no language data from this period, and even the island names we have come from the contact period, a thousand years after Barrancoid settlement. On the basis of our copious Windward Island language data from the contact period, however, it is clear that the language spoken then was a Northeast Maipuran tongue very closely related to the Lokono language of the Guianas, as discussed in Chapter 2 (Breton 1647, 1665, 1666, 1667; Taylor 1977). By inference from that data to the past, the language of Barrancoid times, which is generally referred to as Eyeri (which translates as 'Human Being'), was beyond doubt the language ancestral to the contact period language.

We can not conclusively say what the language of the Leeward Islands was. The archaeological data indicate a primary cultural affiliation with eastern Puerto Rico and artifactual traits of Puerto Rican and Hispaniolan origin, but there are also many traits of Barrancoid and Troumassoid inspiration, if not origin. Inasmuch as the Greater Antillean traits dominate, the most logical assumption is that the language spoken was Northwest Maipuran Taíno, but, given the Windward contribution to the cultures of the area, probably strongly influenced from 500 A.D. on by the Northeast Maipuran speech of the latter islands. Allaire (1987, 1997b:184–185) addresses this question—the ethnic identity of the inhabitants of the Leeward Island Frontier—but a definitive answer is still elusive.

Archaeologically, the Troumassoid cultures of the Windwards were followed in the years between 1000–1450 A.D. by cultures called Suazoid after the Savanne Suazey type-site on Grenada (Bullen 1964). Suazoid ceramics, limited to the Windwards as were the Troumassoid wares, are clearly a development from Troumassoid wares, and it therefore seems certain that they were manufactured by the same population responsible for Troumassoid ceramics. There are, however, some indications that Suazoid wares were influenced by the Greater Antillean wares of the time—Elenan and Chican Ostionoid wares (see Chapter 4)—but this is not surprising considering the fact that we know there were Taíno outpost settlements in the Leeward Islands at this time, specifically at the Salt River site on St. Croix (Morse 1997) and the Kelby Ridge site on Saba, which dates to approximately 1300 A.D. (Allaire 1997a:26, Hofman and Hoogland 1991). Suazoid wares were not manufactured after approximately 1450, and, from the archaeological record, a rather abrupt change seems to have taken place in the overall lifeways of the Windward peoples.

THE PROTO-HISTORIC AND HISTORIC PERIODS

The change is the historically well-documented expansion of Carib peoples from the Guianas into the islands around 1450 A.D. As David Watters (2001:92) has pointed out, contact period documents can reveal considerable important data on the peoples of the pre-Columbian Antilles, and the sociocultural changes in the Windward Islands taking place at this time are a case in point. While one might expect there to be considerable Spanish archival data, there is in fact very little, inasmuch as governmental sources felt that the Lesser Antilles provided no incentive for settlement—there was no gold, they were too densely forested for ranching, and their inhabitants were considerably more bellicose than the Taíno (Ewen 2001:8; McAlister 1984:138). Rather detailed ethnological differences between the inhabitants of the Windward and Leeward Islands, however, were noted by Dr. Diego Álvarez Chanca, who accompanied Columbus on his second voyage in 1493, and additional information comes from letters written by Michele de Cuneo, Juan Coma, and Nicolò de Syllacio, crewmen on that voyage (Chanca 1949; Columbus 1988). Two hundred years later, with the French acquisition and settlement of the Windwards in 1635, we are suddenly flooded with copious information, most of it published, and the peoples of the Windwards leave the realm of pre-history and become part of history.

French documentation comes largely from French clerics, all describing the people who came to be called *Island Caribs* in considerable detail, including those peoples' own remembrance of their immediate past and the arrival of the Carib invaders, as well as detailed descriptions of the language spoken by the inhabitants of the Windward Islands in the mid-1600s (Boucher 1992; Breton 1647, 1665, 1666, 1667; Delpuech 2001; Du Tertre 1667; Howard and Howard 1983; Hulme 1992; Hulme and Whitehead 1992; Labat 1979; Lafleur 1992; Moreau 1988, 1991, 1992; Sued Badillo 1978; Yacou 1992; Yacou and Adelaide-Merlande 1993).

The documentary evidence of change is substantiated by the archaeological record, though that record is sparser for the period after 1450 A.D. than for earlier periods. Suazoid wares, as we have said, were no longer made after about 1450. In their place we find a ware called Cayo ware, so far known only from St. Vincent, in a style not derivative from the Barrancoid-Troumassoid-Suazoid tradition (Boomert 1985, 1986). Future archaeological research on the protohistoric period will undoubtedly clarify the origins of Cayo ware and its distribution in the Windward Islands, but its similarities to the Carib wares of the Guianas are noticeable (Boomert 1985). The combination of documentary and archaeological data make it clear that after 1450 we are dealing with a "new regime," and language data play a large role in its definition.

That there was language continuity from first Spanish contact times to the advent of the French in 1635 is demonstrated by the use of identical island names in both time periods—*Turuqueira*, for example, for Guadeloupe is used both by Anghiera in the early 1500s and by Breton in the mid-1600s (Allaire 1997b:179). In the mid-1600s, the people called themselves *Kalina*, or *Karina*, a mainland Guiana Karina Carib form meaning 'Manioc-Eaters' (Taylor 1977:25), and they identified themselves with the Carib tribe of that name in the Guianas (Allaire 1997b:180). The language itself was referred to as *Kalínago* (usually spelled Callinago) and as *Kalíphuna* (usually spelled Callipuna) by the Island Carib. By a 1660 treaty, the Island Carib Kalínago/Kalíphuna people were largely limited to the islands of St. Vincent and Dominica, and their decline progressed rapidly. On Dominica there were only 125 surviving speakers of the language in 1853 (Thomas 1953), and by 1879 only a few elderly men and women still spoke the language (Ober 1879:447). The last speaker on Dominica died about 1920 (Taylor 1977:24), but the language, though no longer spoken by those who live on the Carib Reserve, is still called *Karífuna* by the surviving Island Caribs of Dominica (Joseph 1997:214).

By the same treaty which forced the Island Caribs to remove to St. Vincent and Dominica, Governor Houël of Guadeloupe allowed those Caribs living on Guadeloupe to remain, though in a small area, far removed from the French (Delpuech 2001:31). Their numbers declined steadily, and in 1825 only seven or eight Carib families remained on the east coast of Grand-Terre. In 1882 only fifteen individuals are reported, and after that all is silence (Delpuech 2001:32–32). The situation on St. Vincent was equally bleak. With the increasing importation of slaves from Africa and consequent intermarriage, usually between Negro men and Carib women, the people became known as *Black Caribs* rather than as Island Caribs. That population fared no better than the Caribs of Dominica and Guadeloupe. By the 1763 Treaty of Aix la Chapelle, France ceded all its Windward possessions except Martinique and Guadeloupe to Great Britain, and the British promulgated an instant policy of "Indian Removal," which between July of 1796 and February of 1797 removed in excess of 4,000 Black Caribs from St. Vincent to the small Grenadine island of Balliceaux. Over half of the people died during that period, and the 2,000-some who survived were shipped in April 1797 to what was then British Honduras, now Belize. The "Island Carib Problem" had been permanently solved on St. Vincent (Gonzalez 1988, 1997). The Honduran exiles, however, prospered in their new homeland, and today there are almost 75,000 speakers of their language, which they call *Garífuna*, in Belize, Guatemala, and Honduras (Gonzalez 1997:119).

THE KALÍPHUNA/GARÍFUNA LANGUAGE

While the exact interrelationships of the languages of the Maipuran branch of Arawakan are still imperfectly known (Wise 1990:89), a thorough examination of the seventeenth-century documentary records on the Kalíphuna language, particularly the grammar and two-volume dictionary of Fr. Raymond Breton, and an examination of Kalíphuna's twentieth-century Central American form,

Garífuna, indicates beyond even a shadow of doubt that Eyeri-Island Carib (Kalíphuna-Garífuna) was not and is not a Carib language, but an Arawakan language belonging to the Northeast Maipuran subgroup to which its closest neighbor, Guiana Lokono, also belongs (Breton 1665, 1666, 1667; Hadel 1975; Rat 1898; Taylor 1951a, 1951b, 1953, 1954, 1955, 1956a, 1956b, 1977). The earliest documented form of the Kalífuna language spoken in the Lesser Antilles on the advent of the French arrival in 1635 differs only in minor lexical details from modern Garífuna speech, the relationship analogous to that between seventeenth-century Shakespearean and contemporary English.

Douglas Taylor and Berend Hoff have demonstrated that in addition to Kalíphuna, spoken by both men and women, a Carib Pidgin was also used by the men (Taylor and Hoff 1980). It was, however, not a language in the usual sense, but, as pidgins are by definition, a language-based verbal short-hand which could be used for minimal communication.

The language of everyday use as recorded by Breton was, like English of the year 1250, a creolized language. Just as the English of 1250 was Germanic in sound and grammar but 30–40 percent of its lexicon altered through the adoption of Norman French words, so Kalíphuna was Arawakan in sound and grammar but had been relexified so that only 33 percent of its vocabulary was of Arawakan origin, 11 percent of Karina Carib origin, and the remaining 56 percent diglossic, in the sense that a male speaker would generally use the Karina word, while a woman would use the Arawakan word for the same item or concept (see Taylor 1977:Chapter 4 [The Vocabulary of Island Carib], p.76, and Chapter 5 [Form and Function of Karina Loanwords], pp. 89–99). Over the years, as fewer Guiana Karina men migrated to the Windwards and each new generation less frequently heard pure Guiana Karina or the Karina pidgin used, the number of Karina loan words in the Kalíphuna vocabulary decreased. Today 77 percent of the vocabulary of Garífuna now consists of words of Arawakan origin, 16 percent of words of Karina origin, and only 6 percent of pairs of diglossic Karina/Arawakan gender-based words. The distinction, that is, between men's speech and women's speech is diminishing (Taylor 1977:76). The reader interested in the details of Kalíphuna and Garífuna grammar is referred to Taylor's *Languages of the West Indies* (1977), which provides a thorough and complete analysis of the sound systems, grammar, and vocabulary of both time-based dialects of the language.

A final note must be added. Karina speakers from the Guianas, of the Galibi tribe, appear to have settled on both Tobago and Grenada sometime prior to European presence on those islands. They were, in any case, living there in 1650 in communities separate from the Kalíphuna people (Allaire 1997b:185; Biet 1664; Pelleprat 1655; Taylor 1977:89).

7

The Toponymic Method and the Derivation of Taíno Morphemes
(With a Note on Macorís and Ciboney Taíno Toponyms)

It is unfortunate, being untrained in and unfamiliar with the field, that so few American archaeologists make use of toponymic data in their studies of human migrations and settlement patterns, unlike their colleagues across the sea, who have over several centuries perfected toponymy to the status of a fine-tuned science. English-speaking Caribbeanists in particular most often dismiss such research with unfortunate and erroneous statements such as "names in traditional societies like the Tainos are notoriously fluid . . . thus the names recorded on European maps . . . were probably in use only during the period of European expansion" (Keegan 1997:29).

And so the matter is ignored, with the implication that place-names change like the wind and are therefore of no use in the reconstruction of historical events and the movements of peoples. In actual fact it has been clear for many centuries in all parts of the world that precisely the opposite is true—that toponyms tend to persist long beyond the lives not only of their creators and users but even of the cultures of which their users were part. Celtic and Anglo-Saxon place-names throughout the British Isles provide one case in point; the toponyms of the American Southeast and Florida provide another; still another can be seen in the place-names of Italy and the Iberian peninsula. The early Celtic peoples; the Angles, Saxons, and Jutes; the Natchez, Tunica, Apalachee, Timucua, Tocobaga, Jororo, Mayaca, Ais, Jeaga, Tequesta, and Calusa peoples; the Etruscans and the Iberians—all have been gone from centuries to millennia, their cultures and languages long replaced by new and totally alien ways of life—but the toponyms they pinned on places survive, perhaps in fractured form, but survive they do, much to the enlightenment of the toponymist and ethnohistorian.

In contrast to this neglect by English-speaking Caribbeanists, Latin American scholars have followed the European norm and have produced five important works on pre-Columbian Antillean toponyms—Alfredo Zayas y Alfonso's monumental two-volume *Lexicografía Antillana* (1931) for Cuba and the Antilles in general; Emiliano Tejera's *Palabras Indíjenas de la Isla de Santo Domingo* (1951) and Emilio Tejera's two-volume *Indigenismos* (1977), primarily for Hispaniola but covering all of the Antilles; Luis Hernández Aquino's *Diccionario de Voces Indígenas de Puerto Rico* (1977, 1993) for Puerto Rico; and Josiah Marvel's *Lucayan Toponymy* for the Lucayan Islands (1988); to which must be added C. H. de Goeje's "Nouvelle Examen des Langues des Antilles" (1939). These volumes contain toponyms totaling well into the thousands, but there have to date been no published attempts to handle that vast body of data with any kind of rigorous analytical techniques.

For exactly that reason the authors began, independently of each other, in the early 1950s, to examine both the surviving Taíno, Eyeri, and non-Taíno, non-Eyeri lexicons and the native place-names of the Antilles with the object of adding to the number of translatable Taíno, Eyeri, and non-Taíno, non-Eyeri forms and of determining the methods by which the Taíno and Eyeri named their settlements. Vescelius in particular devoted an extraordinary amount of time and research over a period of many years to these endeavors, and the bulk of the work reported in this volume on that topic is attributable to his rigorous long-term study. In the late 1970s we began to consolidate our research efforts, and, after Vescelius's untimely death some years later, when most of his linguistic and toponymic notes were turned over to Granberry, the final process of completing our joint venture was begun, resulting in this volume.

The method of toponymic analysis we derived, which owes its origins to the British and European toponymists, is simple and straightforward. The first step is, of course, to list all of the documented non-European current and past-use-only place names of the Antilles. These were recorded in their original orthography. The toponyms were then phonemicized according to the phonemic systems of sixteenth and seventeenth century Spanish and French, the languages in which they were composed, to provide a normalized orthography. The phonemic transcriptions themselves were then rewritten phonetically in order to account for the allophones (phonetic varieties) of each phoneme, enabling the data to be handled from as accurate a phonological base as possible.

In these orthography-phoneme-allophone conversions it was necessary to take into account the fact that none of those who wrote the native forms were speakers of the languages in question, and many, if not most, were relatively uneducated. The exceptions to this statement would have been men such as Ramón Pané, Bartolomé de las Casas, and Gonzalo Fernández de Oviedo y Valdez in the Greater Antilles, and, in the Lesser Antilles, Raymond Breton, but they were not responsible for the form in which most native place-names were written by the colonial authorities.

For the Eyeri toponyms of the Lesser Antilles, the problem of interpretation of toponymic spellings is readily solved by the fact that we have accurate detailed phonemic and allophonic data from modern Garífuna (Taylor 1951a) and from recent and earlier speakers of Kalíphuna on Dominica and St. Vincent (Breton 1665, 1666, 1667; Taylor 1951b, 1953, 1954, 1955, 1956a, 1956b, 1956c, 1958a, 1958b, 1977; Taylor and Hoff 1980; Taylor and Rouse 1955).

The situation for the Taíno and earlier non-Taíno toponyms of the Greater Antilles is, of course, considerably more complex, inasmuch as none of the Greater Antillean languages survived beyond the mid-1500s. One must therefore resort to an interpretation of such toponymic spellings from the point of view of our knowledge of the phonemes and allophones of sixteenth century Spanish. Taking this into account, Spanish form-initial written <b>, representing phonetic [b], was transcribed as <b>, but form-internal, intervocalic <b>, representing phonetic [ß], was normally transcribed as <w>. The <bu> combination was always transcribed as <w>. The letter <c> before vowels <e> or <i> was transcribed as <s>, not <θ>, inasmuch as the majority of the Spanish settlers in the Greater Antilles were of Andalusian origin and would not have used the Castilian [θ] pronunciation of that letter. When before <a>, <o>, or <u>, letter <c> was transcribed as <k>. <Qu> before <e> or <i> was also transcribed as <k>, but before other vowels as <kw>. Letter <g> before vowels <e> and <i> was transcribed as <h>; when before <a> or <o> as <g>. The <gu> combination was transcribed as <g> when before vowels <e> and <i>, and as <gw> before <a> or <o>. <J> and <h> were both transcribed as <h>, except that <hu> was always transcribed as <w>. Both <s> and <z> were transcribed as <s>—again the Castillian dialect [θ] pronunciation was not likely to have been used by the Spanish settlers of the Antilles. The letter <x> poses something of a problem in that its precise phonetic value in sixteenth century Spanish could fluctuate between [h], [s], and [š] as in English *shall*. No attempt has consequently been made to state its phonetic/phonemic status, and it has simply been left as <x>, though when form-initial or form-final, <x> was usually interpreted as [h] and written in our transcription as <h>. The decision on its transcription was based on the morpheme-internal characteristics of the form and the phonetic nature of its cognates, if any, in related Northern Maipuran Arawakan languages.

Vowels <a> and <i> have been left as they are—<a> and <i>. Vowel <e> was generally transcribed as <e>, defined as simple mid front unrounded vowel [ɛ] as in English *met*, but it was transcribed as <é>, defined as higher-mid front unrounded vowel [e], in those environments in which that sound would have occurred in Spanish. The latter phone is rather frequently indicated by orthographic <ei> or, when form-final, <ey> in the original source toponyms. In recurrent syllables where orthographic <o> is sometimes found and orthographic <u> sometimes found in the originals, a <u> has been used. Recurrent syllables which always contain only <o> or only <u> retain those symbols as <o> and <u> respectively. An orthographic <u> or <o> directly following <o> or <u> was interpreted as <-wu-> or <-wo-> respectively. An orthographic <u> or <o> directly following <e> or <i> was interpreted as <-yu-> or <-yo-> respectively. Similarly an intervocalic orthographic vowel <e> or <i> following <e> or <i> was interpreted as <-ye-> or <-yi-> respectively. Finally, there are many instances in which, on the basis of internal phonological patterning, orthographic <n> seems clearly to indicate not a "full" [n] sound, but rather that the preceding vowel was nasalized, a phenomenon not present in Spanish. Such vowels have been rendered with the symbols <ã>, <ẽ>, <ĩ>, <õ>, and <ũ>. In those instances in which internal phonological evidence and comparative morphological evidence does not indicate that the preceding vowel was nasalized, the <n> was left as <n>. A fuller discussion of the probable reconstituted phonemes of Taíno and the transcription of Taíno forms from their Spanish orthography is given in Chapter 9, "Some Principles of Taíno Grammar."

The next step in the analytical process was to arrange the toponyms alphabetically according to their phonetic transcription from the Spanish or French original. Then each toponym was divided into syllables, allowing no two consonants to come together as a cluster, inasmuch as this does not occur in the majority of Arawakan languages in general and Northern Maipuiran languages in particular. The allowed syllable shapes were V, CV, and VCV. These phonological shapes were isolated out as possible individual morphemes, investigated in a later step in the process, as were multiple recurring syllables in a sequence.

Each recurring syllable, usually in Arawakan canonical V, CV, or VCV form, was phonetically written, and the syllabified toponym was entered in a columned grid, as shown in Table 3 below, which provides a sample of selected Taíno toponyms and their transcription and syllabification. In the syllabification grid, each syllable occupies a single column in the row on which the toponym is entered. Syllables which recur in the same position in one toponym after another are placed in the same column and the position of the syllables fore and aft adjusted accordingly on the grid. The toponyms analyzed so far (approximately 1,500) show a maximum grid length of fifteen syllable positions.

All toponyms containing a given recurring syllable pattern were then examined in terms of their geographical location. Where possible, recurring geographical commonalties were isolated as the probable meaning of the syllable or syllables. Each such syllable(s) + meaning group was then checked in the lexicons of all known Arawakan languages for which lexicons or other pertinent publications are available as well as against the few publications on reconstructed Proto-Maipuran and Proto-Arawakan (Matteson 1972; Noble 1965;

Table 3. A Sample Toponymic Analysis Grid

Name	Phonetic	Syllable Position													
		1	2	3	4	5	6	7	8	9	10	11	12	13	14
Abacoa	[a-ba-ku-wa]						a	ba		ko			wa		
Bagua	[ba-wa]							ba					wa		
Baguana	[ba-wa-na]							ba					wa	na	
Bayaguana	[ba-ya-wa-na]							ba				ya	wa	na	
Caguana	[ka-wa-na]		ka										wa	na	
Canabacoa	[kā-a-ba-ku-wa]	kā					a	ba		ko			wa		
Cayacoa	[ka-ya-ko-wa]		ka	ya						ko			wa		
Dabiagua	[da-bi-ya-wa]				da	bi						ya	wa		
Damajagua	[da-ma-ha-wa]				da				ma		ha		wa		
Habana	[a-ba-na]						a	ba						na	
Magua	[ma-wa]								ma				wa		
Maguana	[ma-wa-na]								ma				wa	na	
Maisí	[ma-isi]								ma						isi

Payne 1990; Taylor and Hoff 1980) to determine if a morpheme with an identical or similar phonological shape and accompanying semological denotation could be found.

TAÍNO TOPONYMIC MORPHEMES

The results of this rather routine investigation have so far been rewarding, for a significant number of such phonological-semological patterns do, indeed, have an Arawakan counterpart, specifically a Northern Maipuran counterpart, thus lending credence to our suggestions concerning the form and meaning of the subparts of individual Taíno toponyms. A list of all translatable toponym subparts/morphemes was drawn up early on (see Table 4 below), and each toponym was given an overall translation by joining the meanings of its individual morphemic parts (see sample Table 5 below).

Table 4 gives the list of the 131 morphemes and morpheme combinations isolated from the data by the method described above. Cognate forms are given, where available, in Island Carib (Kalíphuna), Lokono Arawak, Goajiro (G), Proto-Arawakan (PA*), Proto-Asháninka (PAsh*), and Proto-Harakbut (PHk*). Proto-forms are from Matteson (1972), and Island Carib, Goajiro, and Lokono Arawak forms are from Taylor (1977). On the basis of this data the toponyms given in Table 3 can be translated as shown in Table 5.

It was, in short, quickly evident that specific morphemes recurring in the great majority of Taíno toponyms referred to direction from some central location. One morpheme, for instance, occurred only in the names of places on the eastern/near end of a geographical space, regardless of the focal point of that space; another occurred only in the names of places on the western/far end of the same space; yet another occurred only in the names of places to the north of the central location, another in names to the south, and yet another in the names of centrally located places. As Vescelius early noted, this analysis provides us with some insights into the Taíno world-view, or, at least, into the way in which they conceived of geographic space. It was this kind of distribution of toponyms which enabled definition of the individual toponymic morphemes and morpheme combinations.

This Arawakan view of space, linking the 'east' or 'near' and the 'west' or 'far' by a central geographical locale which was often, in coastal locations, a water passage between islands, interestingly supports Irving Rouse's original definition of Antillean culture areas from an archaeological base—the *Vieques Sound Area,* the *Mona Passage Area,* and the *Windward Passage Area* (Rouse 1951). These areas are, of course, reflected in the ultimate distribution of the *Eastern Taíno* (Vieques Sound Area), the *Classic Taíno* (Mona Passage Area), and the *Western Taíno* (Windward Passage Area) and in what Rouse has defined as *Cul-*

Table 4. Taíno Toponymic Morphemes and Morpheme Combinations

Phonetic Form	Source Form	Meaning	Island Carib	Lokono	Other Forms
aba	*<aba>*	first		aba	PAsh *(a)pa 'one'
abana	*<abana>*	lesser of the foremost			PAsh *(a)pa 'one'
ai	*<ai->*	far(ther), west(ern), near distance		iá-	PA *(w)ã-yu; *-ya 'to, from'
aná	*<aná>*	foreland, headland			
ané	*<ané>*	foreland, headland			
ara	*<ara>*	tree, wood	ará-	adda -	PA *aha-
asu	*<asu>*	sunset, western			
ati-	*<atí->*	center, central			
awu	*<abu>*	height(s), highland(s)			
ayai-	*<ayai->*	farthest, westernmost			PA *-ma-
ba-	*<ba->*	big, great, large			
bā-	*<ban->*	biggest, largest, greatest			
baha	*<baha->*	bigger, larger, greater			
baté	*<batey>*	plaza			
bawa	*<bagua>*	ocean, sea	balánna	baráia	PA *para-na/wa
baya-	*<baya->*	bigger, larger, greater			
bi-	*<bi->*	savage(s), wild			
bibi-	*<bibi->*	savages (many)			
bisa-	*<bisa->*	unsettled, forested			
bo	*<bo>*	house, home, dwelling, place		ba-	PA *pa
bŏ	*<bon->*	river			PA *-po-
bohi	*<bohí->*	house, dwelling, shelter			PA *pa
bohiyo	*<bohio>*	househholders			

Continued on the next page

Table 4. Continued

Phonetic Form	Source Form	Meaning	Island Carib	Lokono	Other Forms
-bori	⟨-borí⟩	home people			
-buko	⟨-buco⟩	large area of land			
bukara	⟨búcara⟩	large rock outcrop			
buwi	⟨buwí⟩	house, dwelling, shelter			
da-	⟨da-⟩	down, lower, southerly			
daha-	⟨daha-⟩	downward, southward			
dai-	⟨dai-⟩	down, southerly			
ha-	⟨ha-⟩	upper, north(ern)		ai-omin	
hã-	⟨han-⟩	uppermost			
hai-	⟨hai-⟩	up(per), northern			
haina	⟨haina⟩	lesser of the upper			
hi-	⟨hi-⟩	near, east(ern)	ia-	iá-	
hutiya	⟨hutía⟩	hutia			
i-²	⟨i-⟩	near, east(ern)		iá-	
isi-	⟨isi-⟩	frontier, headland, headwaters			
iti-	⟨iti-⟩	upland, hills			
itku-	⟨itcu-⟩	valley			
ka-¹	⟨ca-⟩	top, north(ern)		-ko	
ka-²	⟨ca-⟩	junction, meeting place			
kā-	⟨can-⟩	uppermost, topmost, most northerly			
kahai-	⟨cahai-⟩	topmost, northernmost			
kai-	⟨cai-⟩	top, north(ern)			

kaiya-	*<caya->*	topward			PA *-ka/e
kasa-	*<casa->*	upstream			
kawa-	*<cawa->*	meeting place			PA *ki-
kawana	*<caguana->*	small meeting place			
kawŏna	*<caona>*	gold	caouánam acáera		
kaya	*<caya>*	island (*ka + ya*)		kaíri	
kayu	*<cayu>*	northern people			
ke	*<que>*	land, island			
kē	*<quen>*	large land, mainland			
keya	*<queia>*	bigger land			
-ko	*<co>*	out(er)		-ko 'far'	
kō-	*<con->*	a planting (of crops)		kúnnuku 'forest'	
kōnuko	*<conuco>*	plantation (*kō+n+uko*)			
kotu-	*<cotu->*	hinterland			
-kowa[1]	*<coa->*	out-country, frontier, shore			
ku	*<co/u>*	friend			
kuba	*<cuba>*	outside(rs)			
kubana	*<cubana>*	lesser outside(rs)			
lu-	*<lu->*	people, group, tribe		lo-	G -yu
ma-	*<ma->*	middle		-mi	
mā-	*<man->*	midmost, most central			
mabo	*<mabó>*	prince			
mabona	*<mabona>*	princeling			
maha	*<maha>*	middle side, midsection			
maka	*<maca>*	end, terminus			
maku-	*<maco/u->*	unfriendly, strange, foreign, barbarous			

Continued on the next page

Table 4. *Continued*

Phonetic Form	Source Form	Meaning	Island Carib	Lokono	Other Forms
makuri	‹macuri(x)›‹	foreigner, enemy			
maniwa	‹maigua›	undergrowth			
mari-	‹marí-›	middle folk			
maya-	‹-maya-›	interior, midwestern			
-misi	‹-misi›	swamp(y) (= 'not sandy')			
mō	‹mon-›	river			PA *-po-
mona	‹mona›	land			PA* mua 'earth'
nakā	‹nacan›	middle (of a place)	ánac	ánnakë	
–na	‹-na›	small			
-ne	‹-ne›	water			PAsh * ni-ha
-ni	‹-ni›	water			PAsh *ni-ha
–ra	‹-ra-›	distant (?)			
-ri-	‹-ri-›	river			
ruku-	‹rucu-›	ridge, mountain range			
sa-	‹sa-›	wood (?)		-da, -so	
saba-	‹saba-›	forest(ed)			
sabana	‹sabana›	savannah (sa + ba + -na)			
si-¹	‹ci-›	sand, rough, hard			PA *-tsi-
si-²	‹-c/si-›	head			
siba	‹ziba›	stone (si + ba)	ichibá	siba	PA *hi-ba-
sibawo	‹sibao›	rocky place (si + ba + wo)			
simu	‹zimu›	face (si- + mu)	ichibou		
-su	‹-su›	sunset, western			PSh *-se

tabuko	‹tabuco›	undergrowth			
-ti	‹-ti›	center, central			PAsh *tsomi
towa	‹toa›	breast			
turé	‹turey›	sky, heaven(s)			
uku	‹ucu›	earth, soil, terrain			PA *kaa-wa-
-uma	‹-uma›	earth		G uma	PA *mua
wa-	‹gua-›	land, country, place			PA *-wa-
wã-	‹gua-›	saltwater, ocean, sea			PHk *wḗëy 'water'
waha-	‹guaha-›	rear, back			
wahana-	‹guahana-›	just to the rear			
wai-	‹guai-›	bottom, southern			
wãni-	‹guani-›	rear-most			
waina-	‹guayna-›	less southerly			
wawa	‹guagua›	free			
waya-	‹guaya-›	farther back			
we-	‹hue-›	hole, basin			PHk *wḗëy 'water'
wiho	‹huiho›	height, mountainous			
-wo	‹guo›	country, land			PA *-wa-
xa-	‹xa-›	water, pool, pond			PA *ni-ha
xama	‹xama.›	bay, gulf, inslet, sound			
xara	‹xara-›	lake (xa- + -ra)			
xawe(i)	‹xague(y)›	natural sink-hole			PA *-ha-re
xawe(ye)	‹xagüe(ye)›	cave, grotto	chaouái	oái-	
ya¹-	‹ya-›	distant, distance, far(ther), west(ern)			
yabā	‹yaban-›	second(ary), another			
yamō-	‹yamon-›	second(ary), another			
yarima	‹yarima›	anus, end, buttocks	árima		

Continued on the next page

Table 4. Continued

Phonetic Form	Source Form	Meaning	Island Carib	Lokono	Other Forms
yaya	\<yaya->	farther			
ye-	\<ye->	coast, edge			
yŏ-	\<yon->	paramount, head chief			
yo-[1]	\<yo->	leading, chief			
-yo[2]	\<-yo>	toward	-u		
yŭ-	\<yun->	higher			
yu-[1]	\<yu->	people, group, tribe		lo-	-yu
yu-[2]	\<yu->	high(er)	-iu		
yuna-	\<yuna->	less high			
yuya-	\<yuya->	higher, heights			

Table 5. Sample Toponymic Translations

Name	Morpheme Constituents	Translation
Abacoa	(a + ba) = aba + ko + wa	First Outer Land
Bagua	ba + wa	Big Land
Baguana	ba + wa + na	Smaller Land (Smaller Big Land)
Bayaguana	ba+ ya + wa + na	Smaller Western Land (Smaller Big Western Land)
Caguana	(ka + wa) = kawa + na	Small Meeting Place
Canabacoa	kā + (a + ba) = aba + ko + wa	First Topmost Outer Land
Cayacoa	ka + ya + ko + wa	Far North Outer Country
Dabiagua	da-bi-ya-wa	Southern Wild Far Country
Damajagua	da + ma + ha + wa	Southern Middle Up-Country
Habana	(a + ba) = aba + na	First Small [Settlement]
Magua	ma + wa	Middle Land
Maguana	ma + wa + na	Smaller Middle Land
Maisí	ma + isi	Middle Headland

tural Frontiers in the progress of Arawakan settlement of the Antilles (Rouse 1951; 1987:Fig. 4, Fig. 6; 1992:Fig. 10).

Such toponyms also seem to indicate the directionality of Taíno movement through the Antilles—from east to west and from 'bottom' to 'top.' The consequent origin point of their migration would seem therefore to be to the east and south of their historic location in the Greater Antilles. There are a few toponyms which define local geographical characteristics, such as lakes or rivers, without any directional reference—*Xaraguá* 'Lake Country', for example—but these are the exception rather than the rule. The method of naming according to associated natural features, however, so typical of Indo-European and something most Europeans assume as "universal logic," is rare in Taíno. Rather, directional toponyms are the norm. Comparison with the place-naming techniques of South American Arawak-speaking peoples indicates that directional-naming is the basic toponymic pattern for the majority of Arawakan languages.

MACORÍS TOPONYMS

For the main islands of Cuba, Hispaniola, and Puerto Rico well over 99 percent of the non-European toponyms have an obvious Taíno source. There remains, however, a small residue of items which have none but highly contrived Taíno or Arawakan derivation. Each member of this residue, given in Table 6, does,

Table 6. Selected Greater Antillean Waroid Toponyms

Island	Toponym	Location	Warao parallel
Cuba	Camujiro	A mineral water area near Camagüey	*ka-muhi-ru* 'palm tree trunks'
	Guara	Settlement in Habana Province	*wara* 'white heron'
	Guaniguánico	Cabo San Antonio region of Pinar del Río Province	*wani-wani-ku* 'hidden moon, moon-set'
	Hanábona	A savannah in Matanzas Province	*hana-bana* 'sugarcane plumes'
	Júcaro	1. River on the Isle of Youth 2. Ranch near Cienfuegos 3. Village near Camagüey	*hu-karo* 'double-pointed, tree crotch'
Hispaniola	Baho	River in the Cibao Valley	*baho-ro* 'shroud, dense (jungle)'
	Bahoruco	Province in the SW Dominican Republic which was heavily forested	*baho-ro-eku* 'within the jungle'
	Mana	River on the south coast	*mana* 'two, double'
	Haina	River on the south coast	*ha-ina* 'many nets'
	Saona	An island off the southeast coast of Hispaniola	*sa-ona* 'full of bats'

however, have a possible parallel in present-day Warao. All of them were first noted by F. Vegamián (1951) and Johannes Wilbert (1957:13–14).

These anomalous toponyms do not follow the Arawakan norm of naming a place according to its position with regard to a central reference point, discussed at greater length in Chapter 6. Rather do they refer to specific geographical or zoogeographical characteristics of the locale in question. Just as review of Guianan place-naming methods helped the authors determine Arawakan naming norms, so a review of Warao toponyms in the Orinoco delta regions today makes it clear that the use of geographic and zoogeographic features in naming places is typically Waraoan. Many of these toponyms refer to coastal, riverine, or alluvial delta characteristics rather than inland geographic features, perhaps a reflection of the fact that Warao settlements have traditionally been located in this kind of environment (Wilbert 1972:65–115).

Anghiera adds the interesting and perhaps pertinent note that he was told by an Indian informant that the river name *Baho*, flowing through the Cibao Valley in Upper Macorís lands of Hispaniola and emptying into the Río Yaque del Norte, was so called in the "ancient language of the land" (Anghiera 1892: IV:195). What, if anything, this cryptic phrase means is unclear, but it might refer to a pre-Taíno, pre-Arawakan language stratum yet remembered by the Taíno.

It is also of interest and importance to note, as indicated on the map in Figure 6, that Greater Antillean Warao-like toponyms are found largely in the ethnically Macorís sections of Hispaniola and in the Guanahatabey region of Cuba. In both instances these possibly residual populations and speech varieties are away from the south-to-north and east-to-west direction of Arawak movement into and in the Greater Antilles. We have dubbed these place-names *Guanahatabey/Macorís* toponyms, in the full realization that this label has yet to be fully demonstrated. It should be noted that place-names with the component *Macorís* 'foreigner, enemy,' in various forms, also indicated on the map in Figure 6, are not limited to the north-central Hispaniolan coast. They also occur on the southeast coast of that island, throughout Cuba, and, quite possibly, as *Morovís,* in north-central Puerto Rico. This would seem to indicate the widespread Antillean distribution of a probably Waroid, certainly non-Arawak, non-Taíno population prior to the advent of the Taíno, without any indication of the numbers or density of such a population.

CIBONEY TAÍNO TOPONYMS

In addition to the Waroid toponyms one also finds a small number of anomalous, clearly Arawakan yet non-Taíno and non-Eyeri, place-names. As we shall see, their linguistic makeup would seem to point toward a third Arawakan presence in the Antilles at some time in the past. The primary examples are the Lucayan island names *Bimini* 'The Twins/The Pair' and *Lucayoneque* (phonologically *lukayunéke*) 'The People's Distant Waters Land,' the name of Great Abaco, which is made up of the morphemes *lu-* 'people' + *ka-* 'northern, upper' + *yu-* 'distant, higher' + *ne-* 'water' + *ke* 'land.'

The common morphemic numeral-indicating form in Arawakan is *pV-* or *bV-*, where *V* indicates any vowel. In words for '2' most Arawakan languages contain this morpheme and a *-mV-* morpheme, which specifically indicates 'duality.' The two morphemes may or may not be linked or separated by various other kinds of designative morphemes. This usage is particularly common in Northern Maipuran languages—Lokono *bíama* '2' with *bi-* 'numeral indicator' + *a-* 'noun-designator' + *ma* 'duality,' for example. Taíno, however, does not use the numeral-indicating morpheme—*yamoka* '2,' where *ya-* is a 'locator' morpheme, plus the normal *mV-* 'duality' morpheme + *-ka,* a verbal suffix. The Lucayan form *Bimini,* however, uses the *bV-* 'numeral-indicator' morpheme, like Lokono and most other Northern Maipuran languages. The name could not, that is, come from a Taíno source, though its source is certainly Maipuran, for while some of the other Northern Maipuran languages use the *ya-* 'locator'

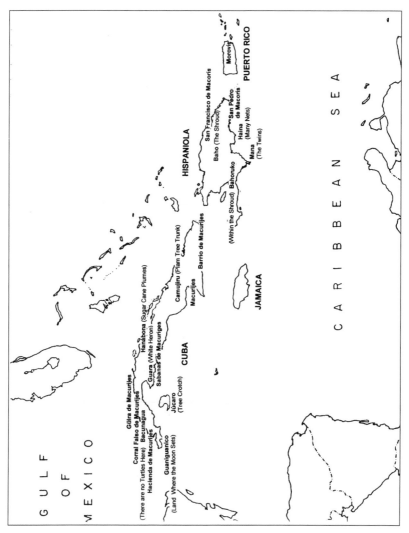

Fig. 6. Waroid Toponyms & Toponyms Containing *Macoris* in the Greater Antilles

morpheme with the numeral '2' as in Taíno, most, as well as the Eastern Maipuran languages, use *bi-* or *pi-* as the 'numeral-indicator' morpheme.

The Bahamian island name *Lucayoneque* is also atypical of Classic Taíno, which does not use the *l-* phoneme form-initially or form-medially. Where other Northern Maipuran languages have *l-*, Classic Taíno has *y-*, as in Taíno *yu* 'tribe, people' and *wayába* 'guava,' Lokono *lo* and *máliaba* respectively. Las Casas points this phenomenon out, indicating that the Lucayans used initial *l-* where the Classic Taíno used initial *y-* in the name of the islands themselves— *"Lucayos, o por mejor decir, Yucayos"* ("Lucayos, or more properly speaking, Yucayos") (Las Casas 1875:III:229). Inasmuch as initial *l-* occurs in all of the Northern Maipuran languages except Taíno and initial *y-* is rare in other Arawakan languages, the initial *l-*becomes-*y* phenomenon would seem to be an innovation limited to Taíno.

These toponymic differences, perhaps minuscule and random to the non-specialist, are telling. They would seem to point toward the presence of two non-Taíno-speaking populations in the Greater Antilles at different points in time. First, to judge from the spread of Waroid toponyms from central Puerto Rico through the far western portions of Cuba, an apparently widely dispersed pre-Taíno Waroid population seems to have inhabited the entire region at one time. Since the Taíno are known from archaeological evidence to have entered the Greater Antilles around the time of the birth of Christ, such a Waroid population must have been long in place prior to that time, gradually displaced by the incoming Taíno.

Secondly, the peculiarities of *Bimini* and *Lucayoneque* hint strongly toward the presence of a third, non-Taíno, non-Eyeri Arawakan population at some as yet unknown time in the past. The archaeological data which impinge on this possibility have been discussed in Chapter 4.

Toponymic analysis can, in short, add interesting and at times important data to historical and archaeological data, enabling a fuller view of a people's past.

8

Toponyms and the Settlement of the Lucayan Islands
A Methodological Test

One of the first tests of the validity and interpretive propensities of the authors' toponymic method was its application to an analysis of the place-names of the Bahamas and the Turks and Caicos, an area of particular concern to the senior author and one in which he has done archaeological work since 1950. A fairly significant number of the aboriginal names of the islands have survived intact to the present: Abaco, Bahama, Bimini, Caicos, Exuma, Guana (in several places), Inagua, Jumento, Mayaguana, and Samana. Abaco and Exuma are now applied to islands other than those they first designated, if we are reading the early maps correctly, but the others still designate the islands they originally named. The names of many others, now replaced by English names, are also known from the writings of the Spanish chroniclers and maps of the early sixteenth century. In all we have 39 aboriginal island names in the Lucayan archipelago (Marvel 1988).

Until recently there has been no attempt to determine what, if anything, Lucayan toponyms meant and what significance such meanings might have in determining the order of settlement, extent of occupation, cultural differences, and relative importance of the individual islands in the archipelago. The names have been listed, of course, with varying degrees of accuracy, and there has been speculation on the import of some of them, but the lack of information on the language of which they were part made even guess-work difficult.

Correlating the native names with specific islands in the archipelago is itself not a simple task, for the early maps often dislocate individual islands and frequently give them shapes which are only partly a function of actual geography. In 1953–1954, using the beautifully reproduced maps of the Duque de Alba's *Mapas Españoles de América, Siglos XV–XVII* (Academia Real de La Historia 1951) and other maps and reproductions available at the P. K. Yonge Library of Florida History at the University of Florida, the senior author correlated the names and locations of the islands in the archipelago from the principal maps of the early sixteenth century, particularly those of Juan de la Cosa (1500), Alberto Cantino (1502), the Turin map (c. 1520), Freducci d'Ancona (1526), Juan Vespucci (1526), and Alonso de Santa Cruz (1545) (Granberry 1955:23–31). Since that time the senior author has also added data from other maps, such as that of Alonso de Chaves (c. 1526). Recently Josiah Marvel has also embarked on a scholarly listing and correlation of 320 cartographic and manuscript sources listing Lucayan island names (Marvel 1988).

The mere reading of the cartographic names, however, is often a difficult task, for variant spellings abound. One is often forced to the assumption that the map-maker himself inadvertently introduced aberrant spellings of individual names, all of which must have been totally exotic and unfamiliar to him. This seems particularly true of maps whose primary task was to chart areas other than the Caribbean itself. Consequently, where individual island names occur in Las Casas's *Historia de las Indias* (1875), that spelling has been taken as definitive, given Las Casas's more than normal familiarity with the Taíno language.

The toponymic method described in the previous chapter was then applied to the 39 surviving aboriginal Lucayan island names. Each name was regularized from its Spanish orthography to a normalized phonetic orthography, and each toponym was broken down into its constituent syllables. Recurring syllables and syllable combinations were then looked at in terms of the meanings given them in the overall toponymic analysis of Greater Antillean place-names, and these meanings were then applied to the resultant constituent morphemes of the Lucayan name forms. The generally monosyllabic morphemes in question are listed in Table 7 below. In the table cognate forms are given, where available, in Island Carib/Kalíphuna (IC), Lokono Arawak (A), Goajiro (G), Proto-Arawakan (PA*), Proto-Asháninka (PAsh*), and Proto-Harakbut (PHk*). Proto-forms are from Matteson (1972), and Island Carib, Goajiro, and Lokono Arawak forms are from Taylor (1977).

The results of application of this analysis to the individual island names is given the Table 8 and the distribution of the names on the map in Figure 7.

TOPONYMIC ANALYSIS

In addition to providing additional data to our store of Taíno morphemes and giving us important data on the manner in which individual morphemes of various types were combined in the Taíno language, the toponymic analysis of Antillean language forms, together with secure knowledge of the location of each name, should give us specific clues concerning the origin and end-points of migrations within the islands and the directionality of such population movements. This is true in the analysis of toponyms from any part of

Table 7. Lucayan Toponymic Morphemes

Taíno	Meaning	Cognate Forms
aba	first	PAsh *(a)pa 'one', A aba
aná	foreland, headland	
ba-	big, great, large	PA *-ma-
bi-	savage(s), wild	
bisa-	unsettled, forested	
bo	house, home, dwelling, place	PA *pa, A ba-
ha-	upper, north(ern)	A ai-omin
hai-	up(per), northern	
hutiya	hutia	
i-²	near, east(ern)	A iá-
ka-¹	top, north(ern)	A -ko
kai-	top, north(ern)	
kaya	island (ka + ya)	PA *-ka/e, A kaíri
kayu	northern people	
-ko	out(er)	A -ko
lu-, yu-	people, group, tribe	G -yu
ma-	middle	A -mi
ma-	not	
-misi	swamp(y) (= 'not sandy')	
-na	small	
-ne	water	PAsh * ni-ha
-ni	water	PAsh *ni-ha
-ra	distant (?)	
sa-	wood (?)	A –da, -so
si-¹	sand, rough, hard	PA *-tsi-
siba	stone (si + ba)	PA *hi-ba-, A siba
-te	far, distant	
towa	breast	PAsh *tsomi
-uma	earth	PA *mua, G uma
wa-, wo-	land, country, place	PA *-wa-
we-	hole, basin	PHk *wëëy 'water'
ya-¹, ay-	distant, distance, far(ther), west(ern)	A oái-
-yo²	toward	IC –u
yu-²	high(er)	IC -iu

the world, but such a predictive propensity is perhaps even greater with the Arawakan languages given the method in which they designed and assigned place-names (discussed in the previous chapter).

From this point of view, by far the most important aboriginal names to us in the Lucayan archipelago are certainly *Inawa* (Inagua) and *Abawana* (Grand Turk). To call Inagua the 'Small Eastern Land' quite clearly implies that it was settled from Cuba, not Hispaniola, since it lies to the northwest of the latter

Table 8. Lucayan Island Names

Spanish Name	Modern Name	Taíno Form	Meaning
Inagua	Inagua	i+na+wa	Small Eastern Land
Baneque	Inagua	ba+ne+ke	Big Water Island
Guanahaní	Little Inagua	wa+na+ha+ni	Small Upper Waters Land
Utiaquia	Ragged Island	huti+ya+kaya	Western Hutia Island
Jume(n)to	Crooked/Jumento	ha+wo+ma+te	Upper Land of the Middle Distance
Curateo	Exuma	ko+ra+te+wo	Outer Far Distant Land
Guaratía	Exuma	wa+ra+te+ya	Far Distant Land
Babueca	Turks Bank	ba+we+ka	Large Northern Basin
Cacina	Big Sand Cay	ka+si+na	Little Northern Sand
Canamani	Salt Cay	ka+na+ma+ni	Small Northern Mid-Waters
Cacumani	Salt Cay	ka+ko+ma+ni	Mid-Waters Northern Outlier
Macareque	Cotton Cay	Ma+ka+ri+ke	Middle Northern Land
Amuana	Grand Turk	aba+wa+na	First Small Land
Caciba	South Caicos	ka+siba	Northern Rocky
Guana	East Caicos	wa+na	Small Country
Aniana	Middle Caicos	a+ni+ya+na	Small Far Waters
Caicos	North Caicos	ka+i+ko	Nearby Northern Outlier
Buiana	Pine Cay	bu+ya+na	Small Western Home
Boniana	Pine Cays	bo+ni+ya+na	Small Western Waters Home
Yucanacan	Providenciales	yuka+na+kā	The Peoples Small Northern [Land]
Ianicana	Providenciales	ya+ni+ka+na	Far Waters Smaller [Land]
Macubiza	West Caicos	ma+ko+bi+sa	Mid Unsettled Outlier
Mayaguana	Mayaguana	ma+ya+wa+na	Lesser Midwestern Land
Amaguayo	Plana Cays	a+ma+wa+yo	Toward the Middle Lands
Yabaque	Acklins Island	ya+ba+ke	Large Western Land
Samana	Samana	sa+ma+na	Small Middle Forest
Yuma	Long Island	yu+ma	Higher Middle
Manigua	Rum Cay	ma+ni+wa	Mid Waters Land
Guanahaní	San Salvador	wa+na+ha+hi	Small Upper Waters Land
Guateo	Little San Salvador	wa+te+yo	Toward the Distant Land
Guanima	Cat Island	wa+ni+ma	Middle Waters Land
Ayrabo	Great Guana Cay	ay+ra+bo	Far Distant Home
Nema	New Providence	ne+ma	Middle Waters
Ciguateo	Eleuthera	siba+te+wo	Distant Rocky Place
Lucayoneque	Great Abaco	luka+ya+ne+ke	The People's Distant Waters Land
Bahama	Grand Bahama	ba+ha+ma	Large Upper Middle [Land]
Habacoa	Andros	ha+ba+ko+wa	Large Upper Outlier Land
Canimisi	Williams Island	ka+ni+misi	Northern Waters Swamp
Bimini	Bimini	bimini	The Twins

island but to the northeast of Cuba. Thus the Cuban origins of Lucayan culture suggested by the most recent archaeological research (Berman & Gnivecki 1991, 1995; Winter and Gilstrap 1991), as well as by the general linguistic data, are supported by this one toponym alone.

On the other hand, to refer to Grand Turk as the 'First Small Country,' *Abawana*, would as clearly imply that it was settled from Hispaniola rather than Cuba, inasmuch as it lies due north of the central coast of that island. The names of the small islands between Hispaniola and Grand Turk, all of which contain the morpheme *ka(y)-* 'top, northern,' and two of which contain the 'mid' morpheme *ma-*, reinforce the assumption. The name of Turks Bank itself, *Baweka* 'Large Northern Basin,' adds further fuel to the fire.

The step-by-step settlement of the central and northern Lucayan Islands from a base on Grand Turk in the east can also be traced by following the directional meaning of the toponyms. We see, for example, that Mayaguana, *Mayawana*, the 'Smaller Midwestern Country,' is indeed to the west of the Caicos. It would have been far to the northeast of the first Cuban settlement, Inagua, so one must assume that Mayaguana was settled by Hispaniolan migrants who had moved on to the north and west from the Caicos. By the same logic, Acklins, *Yabake*, 'Large Western Land,' would seem to have been settled by Hispaniolans on the Grand Turk route, rather than by Cubans from the Inagua route, inasmuch as Acklins is east of the Inagua path but west of the Grand Turk path. From Mayaguana for the Hispaniolans and from Long Island or Exuma for the Cubans, the route seems to have been toward the middle islands and then north.

Cuban settlement from Inagua seems to have proceeded to Little Inagua, *Guanahaní*, 'Smaller Land of the Upper Waters,' and from there likely to the Ragged Island and Jumento Cays chain, the *Haomate*, 'Upper Land of the Middle Distance.' Ragged Island itself was named not directionally but for its apparent abundance of hutía as 'Western Hutía Island,' *Hutiyakaya*. From there the Cuban migrants also headed toward the 'middle,' toward either Long Island, *Yuma*, the 'Higher Middle Land,' and Exuma, *Korateo*, the 'Outer Far Distant Land.' The use of the *luka-* morpheme, meaning 'people' for Abaco, as *Lukayaneke*, the 'People's Distant Waters Land,' rather than the *yuka-* form expected in Classic Taíno, would imply that Abaco was settled first by the Cubans. Bimini, too, would have seen Cuban settlement first, since its name cannot be derived from Classic Taíno, but, rather, from Ciboney Taíno forms.

The map in Figure 7 indicates putative migration routes with solid connecting lines between islands indicating the path from Cuba, commencing sometime in Ostionan times in the 700s A.D., and dotted connecting lines between islands indicating the route from Hispaniola, first sometime during Meillacan times in the 800s A.D. and again during Chican times in the 1200s. In both

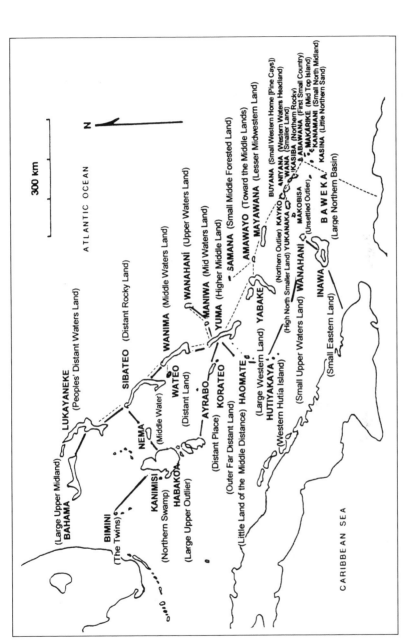

Fig. 7. Toponyms & the Settlement of the Lucayan Islands

LUKAYANEKE (Peoples' Distant Waters Land)

SIBATEO (Distant Rocky Land)

WANIMA (Middle Waters Land)

WANAHANI (Upper Waters Land)

MANIWA (Mid Waters Land)

YUMA (Higher Middle Land)

SAMANA (Small Middle Forested Land)

AMAWAYO (Toward the Middle Lands)

MAYAWANA (Lesser Midwestern Land)

BUYANA (Small Western Home [Pine Cays])

ANYANA (Western Waters Headland)

WANA (Smaller Land)

KASIBA (Northern Rocky)

ABAWANA (First Small Country)

MAKARIKE (Mid Top Island)

KANAMANI (Small North Midland)

KASINA (Little Northern Sand)

BAHAMA (Large Upper Midland)

BIMINI (The Twins)

KANIMISI (Northern Swamp)

HABAKOA (Large Upper Outlier)

NEMA (Middle Water)

WATEO (Distant Land)

AYRABO (Distant Place)

KORATEO (Outer Far Distant Land)

HAOMATE (Little Land of the Middle Distance)

YABAKE (Large Western Land)

HUTIYAKAYA (Western Hutia Island)

KAYKO (Northern Outlier)

YUKANAKA (High North Smaller Land)

WANAHANI (Small Upper Waters Land)

MAKOBISA (Unsettled Outlier)

INAWA (Small Eastern Land)

BAWEKA (Large Northern Basin)

ATLANTIC OCEAN

CARIBBEAN SEA

N

300 km

instances, it is not at all improbable that contact with both Cuba and Hispaniola was ongoing—more archaeological data from the Lucayan Islands is
sorely needed to answer this question. Present archaeological data would seem
not so much to be in agreement with the migration sources and routes suggested here as not to be in disagreement. It is obviously important both to refine
the toponymic data and its linguistic interpretation and to correlate those data
with considerably more genuinely substantive archaeological work in the Lucayan Islands than has been done to date.

9

Some Principles of Taíno Grammar

While nothing has survived in the way of lengthy utterances in the Taíno language, we do have sufficient material to enable us to outline some of the characteristics of Taíno grammar and, by analogy with Island Carib/Kalíphuna, Lokono, Goajiro, and other Northern Maipuran languages, to infer other grammatical patterns which likely typified the language. This information comes from an examination of both the orthography and form of the surviving toponyms and other words in the Taíno lexicon.

The methods used to bring at least some life to this otherwise long-vanished language are those which the late Mary Haas referred to as "reconstitution" (personal communication, Mary Haas 1954; Broadbent 1957). Inasmuch as the only data available are written data, it is necessary to know in considerable detail the correspondence between specific orthographic symbols and the phonological units of the language of its users, in this case sixteenth-century Spanish. From that base it is possible to reconstitute the phonetic system of the language for which the orthography was used, in this case Taíno, and to determine with a high degree of reliability how those phonetic units came together to form that language's phonemic system.

Once the language forms in question have been reconstituted phonologically, an examination of their internal structure by normal methods of morphological analysis enables the definition of morphemes and their allomorphs, as we have discussed in the chapter on toponymic method. A determination of the combinatory patterns of specific morphemes and groups of morphemes, and where possible full words, adds further data to a determination of the tactical patterns of the language in question.

In most cases it is possible to demonstrate that specific grammatical characteristics of Taíno correspond to similar, at times identical, patterns in other closely related Northern Maipuran Arawakan languages, particularly Island Carib/Kalíphuna, Lokono, and Goajiro.

THE PHONOLOGICAL SYSTEM OF CLASSIC TAÍNO

The relatively regular and stable use of alphabetic symbols in the writing of sixteenth-century Spanish makes the task of determining the phonemes which each symbol represented not difficult. There are some minor problems, but these can be handled without undue concern.

We have ample documentary data to indicate the sounds for which alphabetic symbols were used in sixteenth-century Spanish. These are the values, shown in Table 9, used in transcribing Taíno forms, as described in some detail in Chapter 7.

The application of these values to the transcription of the surviving lexical data of Classic Taíno enables definition of the reconstituted phones as shown in Table 10.

Nasalized vowels ã, ẽ, õ, rarely ĩ and ũ, also occur, and nasalization itself was clearly phonemic, inasmuch as it is used to differentiate between the ordinary degree of what we would term an adjective and what we call the superlative of the same form, as in *ba* 'large' and *bã* 'largest.'

With each new Taíno word he cites, Las Casas is usually very careful to indicate which syllable bears strong stress, and Oviedo frequently does so as well. For this reason it is possible to say that stress itself does not seem to have been phonemic in Taíno. Generally speaking, the chroniclers wrote Taíno words and used the acute accent (´) to stress syllables which did not abide by the Spanish rules of accentuation—last syllable if the word ended in a consonant other than *n* or *s,* the next to last syllable if the word ended in a vowel, with exceptions indicated by the acute accent mark. From these orthographic rules, it seems evident that primary stress normally fell on the next to last syllable, but on the final syllable of a multisyllabic word which ended in [e], [i], or one of the nasalized vowels, as in *Manatí, burén* ('griddle'), *Maniabón.* Syllable-final stress also seems to be indicated fairly frequently by use of a final orthographic <x>, which may or may not have been pronounced, as indicated earlier, as a phonetic [h]. Such stress statements are, however, admittedly problematic. Taíno nonphonemic stress, though, would be in keeping with the Northern Maipuran norm.

The symbols in the table of reconstituted sounds are phonetic—they represent, that is, the sounds the Spanish recorders thought they heard in Taíno speech. We do not have enough data of the kind needed to suggest a fully reliable phonemic analysis, though by analogy with Lokono, Island Carib/Kalíphuna, Goajiro and other Northern Maipuran Arawakan languages each of the phonetic symbols would also seem to represent an individual phoneme, with the possible exception of [d] and [r] on the one hand and [u] and [o] on the other. Phone [d] occurs only form-initially, and phone [r] occurs only

Table 9. Symbol-to-Phone in Sixteenth-Century Spanish

Symbol	Phoneme		Phone	Technical Description/Environment/Pronunciation
<a>	=	/a/	[a]	Low central unrounded. All environments. As in modern Spanish (English *father*)
<e>	=	/ɛ/	[ɛ]	Lower-mid front unrounded. All environments. As in modern Spanish (English *met*)
		/e/	[e]	Higher-mid front unrounded. As in modern Spanish (English *fate*, without the glide)
<i>	=	/i/	[i]	High front unrounded. All environments. As in modern Spanish (English *machine*)
		/y/	[y]	Voiced medio-palatal semivowel. When between vowels, and occasionally when form-initial before another vowel, the <i> symbol usually represents phonetic [y] in sixteenth-century Spanish
<o>	=	/o/	[o]	Higher-mid back rounded. As in modern Spanish (English *go*, without the glide)
		/ɔ/	[ɔ]	Lower-mid back rounded. All environments. As in modern Spanish (English *caught*)
<u>	=	/u/	[u]	High back rounded. All environments. As in modern Spanish (English *rule*)
		/w/	[w]	Voiced bilabial semivowel. When between vowels, and occasionally when form-initial before another vowel, the <u> symbol usually represents phonetic [w] in sixteenth-century Spanish
<b>	=	/b/	[b]	Voiced bilabial stop. Form-initial, after nasals. As in modern Spanish (English *boy*)
			[β]	Voiced bilabial spirant. All other environments. As in modern Spanish (no English equivalent)
<bu>	=	/w/	[w]	Voiced bilabial semivowel. When this combination of orthographic symbols occurs before another vowel, it seems invariably to have represented what to an English speaker would be heard as a /w/.
<c>	=	/k/	[k]	Voiceless medio-velar stop. Before /a/, /o/, /u/. As in modern Spanish (English *cat*)
		/s/	[s]	Voiceless apico-dental spirant. Before /e/ and /i/ As in modern Andalusian and Latin American Spanish (English *see*)
<ch>	=	/č/	[č]	Voiceless palatal affricate. As in modern Spanish (English *church*) This sound does not occur in Taíno, and the <ch> symbol is not used by any of the chroniclers who spoke Spanish as their native language, but Anghiera (Peter Martyr), a native speaker of Italian, does use the <ch> orthographic symbol for phonetic [k] (<ch> = [k] in Italian orthography. In all Taíno words recorded by Anghiera that symbol is to be interpreted as the equivalent of Spanish <c> before <a>, <o>, or <u> and <qu> before <e> or <i>

Table 9. *Continued*

Symbol		Phoneme	Phone	Technical Description/Environment/Pronunciation
⟨d⟩	=	/d/	[d]	Voiced apico-dental stop. Form-initial, after nasals. As in modern Spanish (English *do*)
			[ð]	Voiced interdental spirant. All other environments. As in modern Spanish (English *the*)
⟨f⟩	=	/f/	[f]	Voiceless labio-dental spirant. All environments. As in modern Spanish (English *flee*)
⟨g⟩	=	/g/	[g]	Voiced medio-velar stop. Before /a/, /o/. As in modern Spanish (English *go*)
		/x/	[x]	Voiceless medio-velar spirant. Before /e/, /i/. As in modern Spanish (English *ha*)
⟨gu⟩	=	/w/	[w]	Voiced bilabial semivowel. Before /a/, /o/. As in modern Andalusian and Latin American Spanish (English *we*)
		/g/	[g]	Voiced medio-velar stop. Before /e/, /i/. As in modern Spanish (English *go*)
⟨h⟩	=	(/h/)	([h])	Generally silent, but in some 16th century Spanish dialects as in modern English *help*.
⟨hu⟩	=	/w/	[w]	Voiced bilabial semivowel. All environments. As in modern Spanish (English *we*)
⟨j⟩	=	/x/	[x]	Voiceless medio-velar spirant. All environments. As in modern Spanish (English *ha*)
⟨l⟩	=	/l/	[l]	Voiced apico-dental lateral. All environments. As in modern Spanish (English *let*)
⟨ll⟩	=	/ll/	[y]	Voiced apico-palatal lateral. All environments. As in modern Andalusian and Latin American Spanish (English *yes*)
⟨m⟩	=	/m/	[m]	Voiced bilabial nasal. All environments. As in modern Spanish (English *me*)
⟨n⟩	=	/n/	[n]	Voiced apico-dental nasal. All environments. As in modern Spanish (English *no*)
⟨ñ⟩	=	/ñ/	[nʸ]	Voiced apico-palatal nasal. All environments. As in modern Spanish (English *onion*)
⟨p⟩	=	/p/	[p]	Voiceless bilabial stop. All environments. As in modern Spanish (English *put*)
⟨qu⟩	=	/k/	[k]	Voiceless medio-velar stop. Before /e/, /i/. As in modern Spanish (English *keep*)
⟨r⟩	=	/r/	[r]	Voiced apico-dental flap. All environments. As in modern Spanish (closest English equivalent = *bitter*)

<rr>	=	/rr/	[rr]	Voiced apico-dental trill. All environments. As in modern Spanish (no English equivalent)
<s>	=	/s/	[s]	Voiceless apico-dental spirant. All environments. As in modern Spanish (English *see*)
<t>	=	/t/	[t]	Voiceless apico-dental stop. All environments. As in modern Spanish (English *top*)
<v>	=	/v/	[β]	Voiced bilabial spirant. Occurs only in noninitial position. As in modern Spanish (no English equivalent)
		/u/	[u]	This symbol is sometimes used by some writers as an equivalent of the <u> vowel symbol
<x>	=	/h/	[h]	Voiceless faucal spirant. Not present in modern Spanish (English *help*). This usage probably represents the primary value of this letter in sixteenth-century Antillean Spanish.
		/s/	[s]	Voiceless apico-dental spirant. As in modern Spanish (English *see*). This usage seems rare in the spelling of Taino forms as well as sixteenth-century Spanish forms.
			[š]	Voiceless medio-palatal spirant. Not present in modern Spanish (English *shall*). This usage, still in vogue in some parts of sixteenth-century Spain, seems rare in the spelling of Taino forms as well as sixteenth-century Antillean Spanish, which was largely of Andalusian derivation.
<y>	=	/y/	[y]	Voiced medio-palatal semivowel. All environments. As in most dialects of modern Spanish (English *yet*). The value [dž] (English *judge*), frequent today in Andalusia and many parts of Latin America, does not seem to be reflected in any of the Antillean writings on the Taíno.
<z>	=	/s/	[s]	Voiceless apico-dental spirant. Usually before /a/, /o/, /u/. As in modern Andalusian and Latin American Spanish (English *see*)

Table 10. Reconstituted Phones of Classic Taíno

Consonants		Bilabial	Palatal	Velar	Glottal
Stops	voiceless	p	t	k	
	voiced	b	d		
Spirants	voiceless		s		h
Nasals	voiced	m	n		
Laterals	voiced		l		
Flaps	voiced		r		
Semivowels	voiced	w		y	

Vowels	Front Unrounded	Central Unrounded	Back Rounded
High	i		u
Mid	e, ɛ		o
Low		a	

form-internally. These two sounds seem, in other words, to be in complementary distribution and therefore perhaps allophones of a single phoneme, which might be symbolized either by /d/ or /r/. Both correspond to phoneme /d/ (phonetic [d]) in Lokono. There is, however, simply not enough data to reach a positive conclusion. Similarly, both orthographic <o> and <u> are frequently used interchangeably, sometimes in different renditions of the same Taíno word. Thus, for example, one finds *bohio* as well as *buhio* for the word 'house.' As Taylor (1969:235; 1977:31–32) has pointed out for modern Lokono, phonetic [o] and [u] are almost in complementary distribution in that language and may, therefore, have constituted a single phoneme in Taíno, which might be symbolized as either /o/ or /u/, probably the former, since [o] occurs with much greater frequency than [u], but there is not a sufficiently large number of instances to state conclusively that all <o>'s occur solely in one given phonological environment and all <u>'s occur in another, mutually exclusive environment. While the suspicion is great that [o] and [u] are allophones of a single phoneme, for the moment at least, the problem must remain unresolved. In the transcriptions of Taíno forms used in these chapters, <u> has been used when only [u] is present in a given morpheme in all of its known occurrences, and <o> has been used when only [o] is present. When there is vacillation, as in *bohio* and *buhio,* the [o] vowel is used, transcribed as <o>, simply because in most such instances there are more recorded occurrences of the given form with the <o> spelling than with the <u> spelling.

Final syllables ending in orthographic <-ei> or <-ey>, phonetic [ei], are represented by *-é* in our transcriptions, inasmuch as comparative morphemic evidence from other Northern Maipuran languages indicates that Taíno morphemes written with Spanish orthographic <-ei> or <-ey> contained phonetic [e], a higher-mid front unrounded vowel, rather than the [ei] diphthong those symbol combinations represent in Spanish.

Syllables in Classic Taíno may have any of the following structures: V, CV, or VCV. Doubled consonants and consonant clusters do not occur. Doubled vowels also do not occur, but it is possible for two vowels to follow each other if they are in separate morphemes, as in *waiba* 'we leave,' in which the first morpheme is *wa-* 'we,' and the second morpheme is *-iba* 'leave.' Individual morphemes may thus begin in either a vowel or a consonant, but they will always, with one seeming exception and two real exceptions, end in a vowel. The seeming exception involves morphemes containing nasalized vowels *ã, ẽ, õ,* rarely *ĩ* or *ũ,* which are uniformly written by the Spanish chroniclers with an orthographic <n> or <m> following the vowel in question, as in *burẽ* <burén> 'griddle,' but the orthographic <n> or <m> is simply a spelling convention, inasmuch as Spanish did not then, and still does not, have vowel nasalization nor a method for indicating it orthographically. The genuine exceptions, however, are: (1) the phone [s] may occur both syllable- and morpheme-final, as in *mahis* 'maize,' spelled both as <mahiz> and <máhici>, and *hibis* <hibiz> 'cassava sifter,' which occurs infrequently and is always spelled in that manner; and (2) the phone [ɛ] occurs morpheme-final in a single suffix, the masculine noun suffix <-(e)l>.

Processes of phonological change, since they are morphologically conditioned in Taíno, are discussed in the next section of the chapter. Generally speaking, however, it may be pointed out that a base form which begins with a vowel will lose that vowel if it is immediately preceded by a prefix. Thus, for example, the combination of the negative/privative prefix *ma-* added to the base form *ahi-* 'tooth' will become *mahi-* as in <mahite> 'toothless,' not *maahi-*; or the attributive/definite article prefix *ka-* added to the base form *ura* 'skin' will become *kara-* as in <kara> 'skin,' not *kaura-*.

THE MORPHOLOGICAL SYSTEM OF CLASSIC TAÍNO

The morphological system of Classic Taíno is considerably more difficult to define. There are, for instance, so few examples of verbal forms that much of verbal morphology can only be implied. We are on somewhat surer ground when it comes to a discussion of nominal forms, however, for the great majority of words cited by the chroniclers fall in this category.

Morpheme Types and Parts of Speech

There were only three types of parts of speech by form in Classic Taíno—inflected *nouns,* inflected *verbs,* and uninflected *particles.* This accords with the norm in all Northern Maipuran languages. Inflected forms are made from *base* forms and *prefixes* and/or *suffixes,* again a Maipuran norm. Base forms are usually monosyllabic. Multisyllabic bases with the form VCV or CVCV do, however, occur frequently. The latter may or may not be frozen compounds of formerly productive individual monosyllabic morphemes—with so little data to work from, it is frequently difficult or impossible to say. In general, words in Taíno are made up of strings of such monosyllabic morphemes, and, because of the normal V, CV form of morphemes, there are many homophonous forms in the language.

In instances in which a morpheme ending in a nasalized vowel, such as -*wõ* 'gold,' is followed by a suffix beginning in a vowel, such as -*abo* 'with, in possession of, characterized by,' an -*n*- infix, which is neither designative, derivational, nor inflectional in function—what is often referred to as an 'empty morph' is placed between the two morphemes, as in <Caonabó> 'Possessor of Gold,' the name of an important Taíno leader—*kawõnabo* (*ka*- 'attributive prefix' + *wõ* 'gold' + -*n*- 'non-designative/non-derivational infix' + -*abo* 'in possession of').

Nouns

Nouns, as in most languages, indicate the names of entities, real or otherwise. They are recognizable because of their actual or potential use of a specific set of designative suffixes and inflectional as well as designative prefixes. The designative suffixes which characterize Taíno nouns (with V indicating any vowel, though most usually an *a* or *e*) are: (1) -*rV,* (2) -*tV,* (3) -*nV,* and (4) nasalization of the form-final vowel. Each of these noun-designating suffixes was probably used with a specific noun class, attested in Proto-Maipuran and many Maipuran languages, such as Asháninca (Campa), as described by Payne (1990:80–81), Matteson (1972: 164–165), and Noble (1965:28). Examples are: Type (1), with the -*rV* designative suffix, <macorix> 'enemy, foreigner'—*makuri* (*ma*- 'negative' + *ku*- 'friend' + -*ri* 'noun-designator'); Type (2), with the -*tV* designative suffix, <mahite> 'toothless'—*mahite* (*ma*- 'negative' + (*a*)*hi*- 'tooth' + -*te* 'noun-designator'); Type (3), with the -*nV* designative suffix, <Guanahaní> 'Small Upper Land'—*wanahani* (*wa*- 'land' + *na*- 'small' + *ha*- 'upper, northern' + -*ni* 'noun-designator'); Type (4), with final vowel nasalization, <Maniabón> 'Distant Middle Waters Land/Home'—*maniyabõ* (*ma*- 'middle' + *ni*- 'water' + *ya*- 'far, distant' + *bo* 'home' + ~ 'nasalized vowel noun-designator').

Nouns also used derivational suffixes to indicate specific refinements of meaning. Though there were probably a large number of these suffixes in Taíno, as in Lokono and Island Carib/Kalíphuna, only five have survived in the attested data: (1) -abo 'with, in possession of, characterized by,' as in <Caonabó> 'Possessor of Gold'—kawō(n)abo (ka- 'noun-designative prefix' + wō 'gold' + -n- 'non-designative/non-derivational connector' + -abo 'in possession of'); (2) -wa 'in the state of,' as in <tureigua> 'heavenly'—turéwa (turé 'heaven' + -wa 'in the state of'); and (3) -hu 'noun-deriving suffix,' as in <buhitihu> 'shaman' —buhitihu (buhi 'shaman' + -ti 'noun-designating suffix' + -hu 'noun-deriving suffix'); (4) -b(u)re 'collective,' as in <yamoncobre> 'four'—yamōkob(u)re (ya-mōko- 'two' + -b(u)re 'collective'); and (5) -no 'pluralizing suffix,' as in <taíno> 'good (people)'—taíno (taí- 'good' + -no 'pluralizing suffix').

Nouns were not distinguished with regard to number or case by form, but they were occasionally distinguished by a gender-indicating inflectional suffix -(e)l, which indicated masculine gender, as in <caracaracol> 'a scabby person'— karakarakol (ka- 'attributive prefix' + (u)ra 'skin' + ka- 'attributive prefix' + (u)ra 'skin' + ko- meaning unknown + -l 'masculine gender'), or <guarocoel> 'grandfather'—warokoel (wa 'our' + roko 'grandfather' + -el 'masculine noun suffix'). There is no non-masculine or feminine gender suffix to match the masculine gender suffix in Taíno. Gender distinctions in Northern Maipuran Arawakan languages in general do not always equate with distinctions between male and female, but, as in many other languages, are assigned according to cultural criteria which are not predictable. We do not have enough examples of gender distinction by grammatical form in Classic Taíno to make any judgment on the nature of such distinctions in the language. With regard to possessive pronoun reference, discussed below, however, a male-female distinction does seem to have been made.

There are no derivational prefixes in the Taíno data, which is largely in keeping with prefixation patterns in other Northern Maipuran languages, where such prefixes are rare (Payne 1990:75–87), and there is only one designative prefix in the attested data; namely, the noun-designative prefix a-, as in aco 'eyes,' ahi 'tooth,' aō 'dog,' ara 'wood, tree.' It is matched by a phonologically identical morpheme with similar function in other Northern Maipuran languages (Payne 1990:79, Taylor 1952:150).

Inflectional prefixes also occur with Classic Taíno nouns. In first position in a word are the possessive pronominal prefixes: da- 'my'; nV- 'his'; ta- 'her'; and wa- 'our'—the other persons are not attested in the data. In second position is the noun-designative prefix a-, described above, and in third position are the general inflectional prefixes ma- privative or negative and/or ka- attributive (= definite article 'the'). Examples are: <datiao> 'my friend'—datiyawo (da-'my' + -tiyawo 'friend'); <nitayno> 'noble' (literally, 'his goodness,' a term the equivalent of the British 'His Highness,' used for upper rank tribal leaders)—

nitaino (*ni-* 'his' + *tai-* 'good' + *-no* 'pluralizing suffix'); <tarima> 'her buttocks' —*tarima* (*ta-* 'her' + (*a*)*rima* 'buttocks'); <guatiao> 'our friend'—*watiyawo* (*wa-* 'our' + *tiyawo* 'friend'); <mahite> 'toothless'—*mahite* (*ma-* 'negative' + (*a*)*hi-* 'tooth' + *-te* 'noun-designating suffix'); <cara> 'skin'—*kara* (*ka-* 'attributive prefix' + (*u*)*ra* 'skin').

Either *-n-* or *-m-* served as what is called a non-deignative/non-derivational infix or "empty morph"—a morpheme with no meaning at all which functions simply to connect what comes before phonologically to what comes after, as in <Caonabó> 'Possessor of Gold'—*kawõ*(*n*)*abo* (*ka-* 'noun-designative prefix' + *wõ* 'gold' + *-n-* 'non-designative/non-derivational connector' + *-abo* 'in possession of'), or <cama> 'Listen!'—*kāma* (*ka-* 'verb-designating prefix' + *ã-* 'hear' + *-m-* 'non-designative/non-derivational connector + *-a* 'verb-designating suffix').

Verbs

A description of Taíno verb morphology is considerably more difficult than description of noun forms, for there are only eight verb bases in the surviving data. Nonetheless, they do provide some data, and the data match with similar verbal structures in related Northern Maipuran languages.

The attested verb base forms are: *-ibá* 'go, leave'; *-hiya-* 'speak'; *ã-* 'hear, listen'; *-rikē-* 'see'; *-ka* 'be/have'; *-ya-* 'do'; *-bu-* 'be important'; and *ka-* 'kill.' All have cognate forms in Lokono, Island Carib/Kalíphuna, Goajiro, and other Northern Maipuran languages (Taylor 1977:132, 135, 139; Payne 1990:79, 107, 198). These forms occur with accompanying pronominal subject inflectional prefixes, verb-designative prefixes, verb-designative suffixes, and pronominal subject inflectional suffixes. The pronominal prefixes which occur in the data are *da-* 'I' and *wa-* 'we.' The sole pronominal suffix is *-wo* 'us.' The verb-designating prefixes are *a-* and *ka-*. The verb-designating suffixes are *-a, -ka,* and *-nV.* Each of these affixes has cognate forms, phonologically identical or similar to the Taíno forms, in other Northern Maipuran languages (Taylor 1952:150–152; Taylor 1977:45; Payne 1990:79, 105, 106).

Examples of these forms are: <guaibbá> 'let us go'—*waibá* (*wa-* 'we' + *-ibá* 'go'); <ahiacauo> 'speak (to) us'—*ahiyakawo* (*a-* 'verb-designating prefix' + *-hiya-* 'speak' + *-ka* 'verb-designating suffix' + *-wo* 'us'); <cama> 'Listen!'— *kāma* (*ka-* 'verb-designating prefix' + *ã-* 'hear' + *-m-* 'non-designative/non-derivational connector + *-a* 'verb-designating suffix'); <guariquen> 'see'— *warikē* (*wa-* 'we' + (*a*)*rikē* 'see'); <daca> 'I am'—*daka* (*da-* 'I' + *-ka* 'be/have'); <mayani> 'don't'—*mayani* (*ma-* 'negative' + *-ya-* 'do' + *-ni* 'benefactive'); <machabuca> 'it is not important'—*makabuka* (*ma-* 'negative' + *ka-* 'verb-designating prefix' + *-bu-* 'be important' + *-ka* 'verb-designating suffix');

and <macaná> 'don't kill'—*makana* (*ma-* 'negative' + *ka-* 'kill' + *-na* 'verb-designating suffix').

Given the fact that the few processes of Taíno verb formation for which we do have evidence are in accord with similar or identical processes in other Northern Maipuran languages, it is probably not far from reality to assume that additional usual Maipuran verb-forming morphemes and processes were likely also present in Classical Taíno.

The Syntax of Classical Taíno

Since only six full-sentences and a number of two- or three-word phrases have survived in the Taíno language data, it is difficult to say much regarding word order. However, as with verbal structures, enough survives to make some general statements, and correlate these with data from other Northern Maipuran languages. It is also possible to arrive at tactical statements on the word level by comparing recurrent combinations of morphemes.

The six sentences which have survived are:

1. <O cama, guaxeri, guariquen caona yari>. 'O, hear, sir, we see gold jewels.' *O kāma, waxeri, warikē kawōna yari.* The individual words in this utterance may be analyzed as follows: *kāma* (*ka-* 'verb designator' + *ā* 'hear' + *-m-* 'connector' + *-a* 'verb designator'); *waxeri* (*wa-* 'our' + *-xe-* 'male' + *-ri* 'noun designator'); *warikē* (*wa-* 'we' + *-rikē* 'see'); *kawōna* (*ka-* 'noun designator' + *-wō-* 'gold' + *-na* 'noun designator); *yari* (*ya-* 'jewel' + *-ri* 'noun designator).

2. <Mayani macaná, Juan desquivel daca>. 'Do not kill [me], I am Juan desquivel' (Not do kill, Juan desquivel I am). *Mayani makana, Juan desquivel daka.* The individual words in this utterance may be analyzed as follows: *mayani* (*ma-* 'negative' + *-ya-* 'do' + *-ni* 'benefactive suffix'); *makana* (*ma-* 'negative' + *-ka-* 'kill' + *-na* 'verb-designating suffix'); *daka* (*da-* 'I' + *-ka* 'be/have').

3. <Dios naboría daca>. 'I am God's worker' (God, his worker I am). *Dios naboriya daka.* The individual words in this utterance may be analyzed as follows: *naboriya* (*na-* 'his' + (*a*)*bo-* 'worker' + *-ri* 'noun-designating suffix' + *-ya* '?'); *daka* (*da-* 'I' + *-ka* 'be/have').

4. <Ahiacauo, guarocoel>. 'Speak [to] us, our grandfather' (Speak-us, our grandfather). *Ahiyakawo, warokoel.* The individual words in this utterance may be analyzed as follows: *ahiyakawo* (*a-* 'verb-designating prefix' + *hiya* 'speak' + *-ka* 'verb-designating suffix' + *-wo* 'us'); *warokoel* (*wa-* 'our' + *-roko-* 'grandfather' + *-el* 'masculine gender').

5. <Guaibbá, Cynato machabuca guamechina>. 'Let's go, it is not impor-

tant [that] our master is upset' (Let us go, irritated not-important our-master). *Waibá, sinato makabuka wamekina.* The individual words in this utterance may be analyzed as follows: *waiba* (*wa-* 'we' + *-ibá* 'go'); *sinato* (*sinato* 'irritated'); *makabuka* (*ma-* 'negative' + *ka-* 'verb-designating prefix' + *-bu-* 'be important' + *-ka* 'verb-designating suffix'); *wamekina* (*wa-* 'our' + *meki* 'master' + *-na* 'noun-designator').

6. <Técheta cynato guamechina>. 'Our master is greatly irritated' (Much irritated our-master). *Teketa sinato wamekina.* The individual words in this utterance may be analyzed as follows: *teketa* (*teketa* 'much'); *sinato* (*sinato* 'irritated'); *wamekina* (*wa-* 'our' + *meki* 'master' + *-na* 'noun-designator').

In addition to these longer utterances, there are a number of shorter phrases which are informative when it comes to defining the order in which words fell in Classic Taíno. Two of these involve the word 'eye' as the main word of the phrase (in English)—<buticaco> *butikako* 'blue-eyed' and <xeyticaco> *heitikako* 'black eyed.' The word *kako* consists of the attributive prefix *ka-* and the word-root for 'eye,' *-(a)ko*. In both phrases the modifying words, *buti-* 'blue' and *heiti-* 'black' are compounded with the main word and come before it.

It is difficult to say with any degree of certainty what order the major components of a sentence fell in Classic Taíno, for we have no indication of the intonation patterns used for any of the six sentences which we have as data. However, the presumed order of elements is SVO (subject-verb-object, as in English) in the sentences we have except for those containing the verb *-ka* 'be/have,' which comes last in the utterance and suggests the order OSV. This, though, is a gross generalization based on a single form, *daka* 'I am' in both of the *-ka* sentences, and thus may or may not be meaningful. In sentences 1 and 4, however, both objects—*caona yari* and *warokoel*—come in utterance-final position. In the two words *caona yari*, we may also have another instance like *butikako* and *heitikako* in which the modifying element comes before the main element, so that *caona yari* might be properly translated as 'golden rock' or 'gold-stone.'

Thus what little we have in the way of connected discourse in Classic Taíno is of little help in defining rules of syntax for the language. More helpful is the order of morphemic elements within single words. There two things are readily apparent: (1) prefix and suffix morphemes always retain their natural position with regard to the base morpheme they are attached to; and (2) free base morphemes may combine in any number to form a compound, and in such combinations modifying morphemes again seem to fall before the morpheme modified, as in the place-name *Mayawana* 'Middle Distance Small Land,' which consists of the three free base morphemes *ma* 'middle,' *ya* 'distance,' and *wa* 'country.' *Wa* has an attached suffix, *-na* 'small,' and therefore forms a natural unit as *wana* 'small country, small land.' Free base morpheme *ma* 'middle' modifies free base morpheme *ya* 'distance,' and comes before it to form the compound *maya* 'middle distance.' Compound *maya*, in turn, modifies *wana* and comes before it, yielding the full word *Mayawana*.

It thus seems clear that within single words compounded from two or more free base morphemes, modifying free base morphemes come before the free base which they modify. Modifying morphemes which are either prefixes or suffixes, especially the latter, never occur by themselves and fall in their normally defined position to modify a free base.

A Short Lexicon of Taíno
Morphemes and Lexical Forms

This lexicon includes both the known primary morphemes of the Taíno language—free bases and affixes—as well as the majority of single and multi-morphemic words which appear in written form in the sixteenth-century Spanish sources, with the exception of toponyms and the names of a large number of unidentified, and unidentifiable, plants. Completion of the analysis of the several thousand attested Taíno toponyms and plant names, a monumental project yet in progress, will undoubtedly add further base morphemes to our inventory as well as the individual place and plant names themselves. Despite this, it is presently possible to provide a list of certainly 98 percent or more of the known primary base morphemes of the language and all of the affix morphemes which have survived in the attested data. They are given in the following table in both reconstructed phonetic form and in their orthography from the original sources. Where possible, cognate forms from other Arawakan languages, primarily Island Carib/Kalíphuna and Lokono, have been added (in their recorded orthographies rather than a phonetic or phonemic transcription). If we have a cognate Goajiro form, that is included (with the abbreviation G), and, where possible, Proto-Maipuran (PM*, after Wise, in Payne 1990) and Proto-Arawakan, Proto-Piro-Apuriná, Proto-Harakbut, Proto-Shani, and Proto-Asháninka cognates (after Matteson 1972) have also been added in the *Other Forms* column (with the abbreviations PM*, PA*, PP-Ap*, PHk*, PSh*, and PAsh*, respectively). The lack of a cognate form does not mean that there is none; rather, it reflects the extremely uneven data and field-work—in amount and reliability—available from Northern Maipuran languages, despite the considerable publication in that field over the past several decades.

Affixes and bases have been given in two separate lists, and affixes have been further separated into prefixes, infixes, and suffixes. Base forms which do not appear alone, but are found only in combination with prefixes and/or suffixes, are indicated by a preceding and/or following dash in the list of bases. Both prefixes and suffixes have been further differentiated according to whether they are designative, derivational, or inflectional. While such a list of morphemes can hardly constitute a dictionary, a two-way listing, Taíno-English and English-Taíno, has been provided in the event the latter might be of use to other researchers.

Table 11. Taíno–English Lexicon

Affixes

Phonetic Form	Source Form	Meaning	Island Carib	Lokono/ Goajiro	Other Forms
Prefixes					
a-	<a->	noun-designator		a-	PM *a-
da-	<da->	my			
ka-¹	<ca->	attributive prefix (the)	ga-	ka-	PA *kV-
ka-²	<ca->	verb-designator			
ma-	<ma->	privative/negative prefix (not)	ma-	ma-	PA *ma-, PM *ma-
nV-	<nV->	his		G n-	
ta-	<ta->	her	t-	th-	
wa-	<gua->	our			PA *wa-
Infixes					
-m-	<-m->	empty morph connector			
-n-	<-n->	empty morph connector			PM *a-
Suffixes					
-abo	<-abo>	with, in possession of, characterized by	-abu	-abo	
-b(u)re	<-bre>	added to, inclusive	-buri		
-el	<-el>	masculine, son of		l-	PA *li-
-hu	<-hu>	noun-deriver			
-ka	<-ca>	verb-designator (transitive)	-ca		PA *-ka, PM *-ka
-n	<-n>	subordinate inflection		-n	
-na	<-na>	little, small			

Continued on the next page

Table 11. *Continued*

Affixes

Phonetic Form	Source Form	Meaning	Island Carib	Lokono/Goajiro	Other Forms
-na[2]	<-na->	*verb-designator*		-na	
-ne	<-ne>	*noun-designator*	-ne		PA *-nV
-ni	<-ni>	*noun-designator*	-ni		PA *-nV
-ra	<-ra->	far from (the speaker)		-ra	
-ri	<-ri(x)>	*noun-designator* (masc., human)	-ri		PA *-ri
-te	<-te>	*noun-designator*		-te	PA *-tV
-wa	<-wa>	*verb-designator* (stative)	-gua		PA *-wa 'intransitive'
-wo	<-wo>	we		-o	

Bases and Full Lexical Forms

Phonetic Form	Source Form	Meaning	Island Carib	Lokono/Goajiro	Other Forms
-ã	<-am->	hear			PA *ke-ma
aba	<aba>	first		aba	PAsh *(a)pa 'one'
abana	<abana>	lesser of the foremost			PAsh *(a)pa 'one'
ahi[1]	<axi>	red pepper			
ahi[2]	<-ahi->	tooth	-ári	-ári	PAsh *ahí
ahiyaka	<ahiaka->	speak (*a + hiya + ka*)			
ai	<ai->	far(ther), west(ern), near distance		iá-	PA *$(w)a^n$-yu; *-ya 'to, from'

-ako	<-aco>	eye			PM *ogi-
ana	<ana>	flower	ácou	akússi	
aná	<aná>	foreland, headland			
anaki	<anaqui>	enemy	ácani	G aínii	
ané	<ané>	foreland, headland			
ara	<ara>	tree, wood	ará	adda - 'tree'	PA *aha-
arabuko	<ar(c)abuco>	woods, forest	arábou	adda - 'tree'	PA *aha-
areite	<areite>	dance, song			
ari(ke)	<ari(que)>	river (?)			PA *-hu
asu	<asu>	sunset, western			
ati-	<att->	center, central			
awõ	<aon>	dog	ánli		
awu	<abu>	height(s), highland(s)			
ayai-	<ayai->	farthest, westernmost			
ba-	<ba->	big, great, large			PA *-ma-
bā-	<ban->	biggest, largest, greatest			
baha	<baha->	bigger, larger, greater			
bahari	<bahari>	lord, great man, sir			
baté	<batey>	plaza			
bateya	<batea>	trough	batáya		
bawa	<bagua>	ocean, sea	balánna	baráa	PA *para-na/wa
baya-	<baya->	bigger, larger, greater			
bayohabawo	<baiohabao>	drum, tambourine			
behike	<behique>	doctor, shaman	ibíẽ	ibihi 'medicine'	
behuko	<bejuco>	vine (be + (h) + uku)			PA *-pi-
bi-	<bi->	savage(s)			
bibi-	<bibi->	savages (in great numbers)			

Continued on the next page

Table 11. *Continued*

Phonetic Form	Source Form	Meaning	Island Carib	Lokono/ Goajiro	Other Forms
biha	*\<bija>*	*Bixa orellana*	bíchet		
bisa-	*\<bisa->*	unsettled, forested			
bo	*\<bo>*	house, home, dwelling, place		ba-	PA *pa
bõ	*\<bõ>*	river			PA *-po-
bohi	*\<bohí->*	house, dwelling, shelter			PA *pa
bohike	*\<bohique>*	doctor, shaman	ibíẽ	ibihi 'medicine'	
bohiyo	*\<bohio>*	householders			
-bori	*\<-borí>*	native people, home people			
-bori	*\<-bori->*	work			
-boriya	*\<-boría>*	work(er)			
-bu-	*\<-bu->*	be important			
-buko	*\<-buco>*	large area of land (*ba* + *uku*)			
buhite	*\<buhiti>*	doctor, shaman	ibíẽ	ibihi 'medicine'	
buhiti	*\<buh(u)iti>*	doctor, shaman	ibíẽ	ibihi 'medicine'	
bukara	*\<búcara>*	large rock outcrop			
burẽ	*\<burén>*	cassava griddle	bouírrêlet	búddali	PP-Ap *po-
buti-	*\<butí->*	blue			
buwi	*\<buwí>*	house, dwelling, shelter			
-buya	*\<-buya>*	rope, cord	câboya	G api	
bVhV-	*\<bVhV->*	doctor, shaman	ibifí	ibihi 'medicine'	
da-	*\<da->*	down, lower, southerly			
daha-	*\<daha->*	downward, southward (*da* + *ha*)			

dai-	*<dai->*	down, southerly (*da* + *i*)			
daka	*<daca>*	I (*da* + *-ka*)		dákia	
dita	*<dita>*	cup, dish, dipper	rita		
duhu	*<duhu>*	ceremonial seat	From Warao *duhu* 'sit'		
ha-	*<ha->*	upper, north(ern)		ai-omin	
hâ-	*<han->*	uppermost			
haba	*<haba>*	basket	hába	hábba	
hahe	*<hage>*	sweet potato		G háliti	
hai-	*<hai->*	up(per), northern			
haina	*<haina>*	lesser of the upper			
haketa	*<haqueta>*	variety of small shark			
hamaka	*<hamaca>*	hammock			PA *amako
hati	*<hatty>*	cayenne pepper	áti	háthi	
hawa	*<xagua>*	genipa	cháoua		
he-	*<-xe->*	male			PA *ha-
heiti-	*<xeyti->*	black (*hei-* + *-ti*)			PA *-saki-
heketi	*<hequeti>*	single, one	ligueti	ikini-	
-heri	*<-xeri>*	sir, lord, man			
hi-	*<hi->*	near, east(ern)	ia-	iá-	
hibis	*<hibiz>*	basketry sifter	hébechet		
hikako	*<hicaco>*	coco plum	icácou	G kaáko	
hiko	*<hico>*	hammock ropes			
hikoteya	*<hicotea>*	small sea turtle			
hiriwawo	*<jiriguao>*	louse			
hiwaka	*<higuaca>*	parrot			
hiwera	*<hibuera>*	calabash (*hi-* + *we* + *-ra*)	huira	iuida	
-hiya	*<-hiya>*	speak			

Continued on the next page

Table 11. *Continued*

Phonetic Form	Source Form	Meaning	Island Carib	Lokono/ Goajiro	Other Forms
hiyẽ	\<hyen\>	manioc juice	ínhali		
hobo	\<hobo\>	*Spondias* sp.	oúbou	hóbo	
hupiya	\<hupia\>	specter	ópoyem		
hurakã	\<huracán\>	hurricane			
hutiya	\<hutia\>	hutía			
i¹	\<y\>	river-grass			
i-²	\<i-\>	near, east(ern)		iá-	
-iba	\<-ibbá\>	leave	-iba	-iiba	PA* -bokʰa
inkayeke	\<incaieque\>	village			
isi-	\<isi-\>	frontier, headland, headwaters			
-ita	\<-ita\>	know (?)			PA* -SI-a
iti-	\<iti-\>	upland, hills			
itku-	\<itcu-\>	valley			
iwana	\<iguana\>	iguana	-yoána	ioána	
ka-¹	\<ca-\>	top, north(ern)		-ko	
ka-²	\<ca-\>	junction, meeting place			
-ka³	\<-ca\>	be, have			PM* -kʰa
-ka-⁴	\<-ca-\>	kill			
kã-	\<can-\>	uppermost, topmost, most northerly			
kabuya	\<cabuya\>	rope, cord	cáboya	G apí	PA* -pi-
kahai-	\<cahai-\>	topmost, northernmost			

kai-	*‹cai-›*	top, north(ern)			
kaimã	*‹caimán›*	crocodile			
kairo	*‹cairo›*	girdle			
kaiya-	*‹caya-›*	topward			
kakawete	*‹cacahuete›*	peanut			
kako	*‹caco›*	eye(s) (*ka-* 'attributive' + *ko* 'eye(s)')	ácou	akússi	PA *ogi-
kakona	*‹cacona›*	glass bead, reward			
kam-	*‹cam-›*	hear, listen			PA *ke-ma
kama	*‹cama›*	hear, listen			PA *ke-ma
-kana	*‹-caná›*	kill			
kané	*‹caney›*	house (rectangular)			
kaniba	*‹caniba›*	Carib Indian	calliponam	kallipina	
kanokū	*‹canocúm›*	three			
kanowa	*‹canoa›*	canoe (*ka-* + *nowa*)	canáoa	kanóa	PA *kanawa
kara	*‹cara›*	skin (*ka-* + *(u)ra*)			
karabuco	*‹carabuco›*	weeds, small trees	arábou	adda - 'tree'	PA *aha-
karobé	*‹carobei›*	cotton plant			PA *-pehi-
kasa-	*‹casa-›*	upstream			
kasabi	*‹cazabi›*	cassava			
kasike	*‹cacique›*	chief (*ka-* + *si* + *-ke*)			
kawa-	*‹cawa-›*	meeting place			
kawana	*‹caguana-›*	small meeting place (*ka-* + *wa* + *-na*)			
-kawe-	*‹-cague-›*	peanut			
kawõna	*‹caona›*	gold (*ka-* + *wõ-* + *-na*)	caouánam		
kaya	*‹caya›*	island (*ka* + *ya*)	acáera	kaíri	PA *-ka/e

Continued on the next page

Table 11. *Continued*

Phonetic Form	Source Form	Meaning	Island Carib	Lokono/ Goajiro	Other Forms
kayu	⟨cayu⟩	northern people			
kayuko	⟨cayuco⟩	small canoe			
ke	⟨que⟩	land, island			PA *ki-
kē	⟨quen⟩	large land, mainland			
kemi	⟨quemi⟩	species of rodent			
keya	⟨queia⟩	bigger land			
-ko	⟨-co⟩	out(er)		-ko 'far'	
kō-	⟨con-⟩	a planting (of crops)			
kohiwisi	⟨cohibici⟩	conch jewels			
kohowa	⟨cohoba⟩	tobacco powder			
kohowo	⟨cohobo⟩	conch			
kokuyo	⟨cocuyo⟩	fire-fly			
komehē	⟨comejen⟩	termite			PA *kamara
kōnike	⟨coniche⟩	belongings			
kōnuko	⟨conuco⟩	plantation ($k\bar{o}$ + n + uko)		kúnnuku 'forest'	
kotara	⟨cotara⟩	sandal			
kotu-	⟨cotu-⟩	hinterland			
-kowa[1]	⟨-coa⟩	out-country, frontier, shore			
kowa[2]	⟨coa⟩	planting stick			
kowo	⟨cobo⟩	snail			
ku[1]	⟨co/u⟩	friend			
ku[2]	⟨cu⟩	temple			

kuba	<cuba>	outside(rs)			
kubana	<cubana>	lesser outside(rs)			
kuri	<curî>	species of rodent	couli	kúri lo- -mi	G -yu
lu-	<lu->	people, group, tribe			
ma-	<ma->	middle			
mã-	<man->	midmost, most central			
mabo	<mabó>	prince			
mabona	<mabona>	princeling			
maha	<maha>	middle side, midsection			
mahisi	<mãhici>, <mahiz>	maize	márichi	márissi	
mahite	<mahite>	toothless (*ma-* + (*a*)*hi* + *-te*)			
maka	<maca>	end, terminus			
makana	<macana>	wooden club			
mako	<maco>	frog			
maku-	<maco/u->	unfriendly, strange, foreign, barbarous			
makuri	<macuri(x)>	foreigner, enemy			
makuto	<macuto>	deep basket			
manati	<manati>	manatee	manáttoui	-mana-	
manaya	<manaya>	stone knife	-mana		
mani	<mani>	peanut	mánli		PAsh *maní-ti 'jaguar' (!)
maniwa	<maigua>	undergrowth			
mari-	<mari->	middle folk			
mariwana	<mariguana>	frog			
matũ	<matum>	generous			

Continued on the next page

Table 11. *Continued*

Phonetic Form	Source Form	Meaning	Island Carib	Lokono/ Goajiro	Other Forms
matúheri	*<matunheri>*	gentleman, lord (*matú + he + ri*)			
mawei	*<maguey>*	drum			
maya-	*<maya->*	interior, midwestern			
mayani	*<mayani>*	don't (*ma- + ya- + ni*)	mani-	mani-	
maye	*<maye>*	mosquito			PA *mei
mekina	*<mechina>*	gentleman, lord, God			
mikina	*<miquina>*	gentleman, sir, lord			
-misi	*<misi>*	swamp(y) (= 'not sandy')			
mõ	*<mon>*	river			PA *-po-
mohi	*<mohi>*	smaller species of rodent			
mokuyo	*<mocuyo>*	custard apple			
mona	*<mona>*	land			PA* mua 'earth'
nahe	*<nahe>*	paddle			PA *-ha-
nakã	*<nacan>*	middle (of a place)	ánac	ánnakë	
-naki	*<naque>*	enemy			
nasa	*<nasa>*	net			
nati	*<nati>*	chest (of the body)			
nawa	*<nagua>*	woman's loin-cloth		G naáwa	
-ne	*<-ne>*	water			PAsh *ni-ha
neibowa	*<neiboa>*	sticky (*ne + i + bo + wa*)			
-ni	*<ni>*	water			PAsh *ni-ha

nitaino	*<nitayno>*	lord (lit 'His Goodness') (*ni- + taino*)			
operito	*<operito>*	spirit of the dead			
opíya	*<opía>*	spirit of the dead			
papaya	*<papaya>*	papaya	abábai	papáia	
-rei-	*<-rei->*	dance, song			
-ri-	*<-ri->*	river			
-rikě	*<-riquen>*	see, look			
-robé	*<-robei>*	cotton plant			
-roko-	*<-roco->*	grandfather	(à)rgouti	(a)dukutti	
ruku-	*<rucu->*	ridge, mountain range			
sa-	*<sa->*	wood (?)		-da, -so	
saba-	*<saba->*	forest(ed)			
sabana	*<sabana>*	savannah (*sa + ba + -na*)			
-sabi	*<-zabi>*	cassava			
sanako	*<sanaco>*	stupid, foolish			
seiba	*<ceiba>*	ceiba tree			
semi	*<zemí>*	god, supernatural spirit	chemíin	sémehe	PA -pehi
sera	*<serra>*	barter, trade, exchange			
si-[1]	*<ci->*	sand, rough, hard			
-si-[2]	*<-c/si->*	head			
siba	*<ziba>*	stone (*si + ba*)	ichibá	siba	PA *-tsi-
sibawo	*<sibao>*	rocky place (*si + ba + wo*)			
sibukan	*<cibucán>*	crate			
simu	*<zimu>*	face (*si- + mu*)	ichíbou		PA *hi-ba-
sinato	*<cynato>*	irritated			
siwa	*<cigua>*	sea snail	chioua		

Continued on the next page

Table 11. *Continued*

Phonetic Form	Source Form	Meaning	Island Carib	Lokono/ Goajiro	Other Forms
siwato	⟨*ciguato*⟩	foolish, stupid			
-su	⟨*-su*⟩	sunset, western			PSh *-se
tabako	⟨*tabaco*⟩	tobacco			
tabuko	⟨*tabuco*⟩	undergrowth			
taino	⟨*tayno*⟩	good			
tawawa	⟨*taguagua*⟩	earring			
-teito-	⟨*-teito*-⟩	be quiet			
teitoka	⟨*teitoca*⟩	be quiet			
teketa	⟨*techeta*⟩	much			
tekina	⟨*tequina*⟩	master, leader			
tereke	⟨*tereque*⟩	utensil, furniture			
-ti	⟨*-ti*⟩	center, central			
tiyawo	⟨*-tiao*⟩	friend	-tiaon		
tona	⟨*tona*⟩	frog			PP=Ap *n-toro 'toad'
towa	⟨*toa*⟩	breast			PAsh *tsomi
turé	⟨*turey*⟩	sky, heaven(s)			
uku	⟨*ucu*⟩	earth, soil, terrain			PA *kaa-wa-
-uma	⟨*-uma*⟩	earth		G uma	PA *mua
ura	⟨*(u)ra*⟩	skin			
wa-	⟨*gua-*⟩	land, country, place			PA *-wa-
wã-	⟨*gua-*⟩	saltwater, ocean, sea			PHk *wêëy 'water'
waha-	⟨*guaha-*⟩	rear, back			

wahana-	⟨*guahana-*⟩	just to the rear			
wai-	⟨*guai-*⟩	bottom, southern			
wäi-	⟨*guani-*⟩	rear-most			
waiba	⟨*guaibbá*⟩	Let us leave (*wa-* + *iba*)	ouáiba	waiiba	
waikan	⟨*guaicán*⟩	remora (fish)			
waina-	⟨*guayna-*⟩	less southerly			
waisa	⟨*guaiza*⟩	mask			
wanabana	⟨*guanábana*⟩	guanabana (*Annona* sp.)	ouallápana	oarafana	
wanĩ	⟨*guanín*⟩	low grade of gold			
wariketẽ	⟨*guariquetén*⟩	wooden bowl			
wasabara	⟨*guazábara*⟩	battle			
wawa	⟨*guagua*⟩	free			
wawana	⟨*guaguana*⟩	weakness in the legs			
wawarei	⟨*guaguarei*⟩	drinking vessel			
waya-	⟨*guaya-*⟩	farther back			
wayaba	⟨*guayaba*⟩	guava			
wayo	⟨*guayo*⟩	grater			PHk *wëëy 'water'
we-	⟨*hue-*⟩	hole, basin	coyábou	máliaba	PA *-wa-
wiho	⟨*huiho*⟩	height, mountainous			
-wo	⟨*-guo*⟩	country, land			
-wö¹	⟨*-on-*⟩	gold	-ouán-ánli		PA *ni-ha
-wö²	⟨*-an-*⟩	dog			PA *ha-re
xa-	⟨*xa-*⟩	water, pool, pond			PA *ha-
xama	⟨*xama*⟩	bay, gulf, inlet, sound			
xara	⟨*xara-*⟩	lake (*xa-* + *-ra*)			
xawe(i)	⟨*xague(y)*⟩	natural sink-hole	chaouái		
xawe(ye)	⟨*xagüe(ye)*⟩	cave, grotto			
-xe-	⟨*-xe-*⟩	male			

Continued on the next page

Table 11. *Continued*

Phonetic Form	Source Form	Meaning	Island Carib	Lokono/ Goajiro	Other Forms
ya-¹	*‹ya-›*	distant, distance, far(ther), west(ern)		oái-	
ya-²	*‹ya-›*	do			
yabā	*‹yaban-›*	second(ary), another	maní-	mani-	
yamõ-	*‹yamon-›*	second(ary), another			
yamoka	*‹yamocá›*	two	biama	biama	
yamõkobre	*‹yamoncóbre›*	four (*yamoka* + *-b(u)re*)	bánbouri	biábite	
yani	*‹-yani›*	do	maní-	mani-	
yari	*‹yari›*	jewel, ornament (*ya* + *-rī*)	íari	-iédi	
yarima	*‹yarima›*	anus, end, buttocks	árima		
yawa	*‹yagua›*	a type of palm	iaoúalia		
yaya	*‹yaya-›*	farther			
yayawa	*‹yayagua›*	pineapple			
ye-	*‹ye-›*	coast, edge			
yõ-	*‹yon-›*	paramount, head chief			
yo-¹	*‹yo-›*	leading, chief			
-yo²	*‹-yo›*	toward	-u		
yū-	*‹yun-›*	higher			
yu-¹	*‹yu-›*	people, group, tribe		lo-	B -yu
yu-²	*‹yu-›*	high(er)	-iu		
yuka	*‹yuca›*	manioc			PA *$ka^n a^n$-ha-SI
-yuko	*‹-yuco›*	small canoe			
yuna-	*‹yuna-›*	less high			
yuya-	*‹yuya-›*	higher, heights			

Table 12. English–Taíno Lexicon

English	Taíno	Source spelling
another	yabā-, yamō-	<yaban->, <yamon->
anus	yarima	<yarima>
back (direction)	waha-	<guaha->
barbarous	maku-	<maco/u->
barter	sera	<serra>
basin (the sea)	we-	<hue->
basket	haba	<haba>
basketry sifter	hibis	<hibiz>
battle	wasabara	<guazábara>
bay	xama	<xama>
be	-ka[3]	<-ca>
be important	-bu-	<-bu->
be quiet	teitoka, -teito-	<teitoca>, <-teito->
belongings	kōnike	<coniche>
big	ba-	<ba->
bigger land	keya	<queia>
bigger	baha, baya-	<baha->, <baya->
biggest	bā-	<ban->
Bixa orellana	biha	<bija>
black	heiti-	<xeyti->
blue	buti-	<buti->
bottom	wai-	<guai->
breast	towa	<toa>
buttocks	yarima	<yarima>
calabash	hiwera	<hibuera>
canoe	kanowa	<canoa>
Carib Indian	kaniba	<caniba>
cassava	kasabi	<cazabi>
cassava	-sabi	<-zabi>
cassava griddle	burē	<burén>
cave, grotto	xawe(ye)	<xagüe(ye)>
cayenne pepper	hati	<hatty>
ceiba tree	seiba	<ceiba>
center	-ti	<-ti>
center, central	ati-	<atí->
central	-ti	<-ti>
central (most)	mā-	<man->
ceremonial seat	duhu	<duhu>
chest (body)	nati	<nati>
chief	kasike, yo-[1]	<cacique>, <yo->
coast	ye-	<ye->
coco plum	hikako	<hicaco>
conch	kohowo	<cohobo>
conch jewels	kohiwisi	<cohibici>
cord	kabuya, -buya	<cabuya>, <-buya>

Continued on the next page

Table 12. *Continued*

English	Taíno	Source spelling
cotton plant	karobé, -robé	<*carobei*>, <*-robei*>
cotton plant	-robé	<*-robei*>
country	wa-, -wo	<*gua-*>, <*-guo*>
crate	sibukan	<*cibucán*>
crocodile	kaimā	<*caimán*>
cup	dita	<*dita*>
custard apple	mokuyo	<*mocuyo*>
dance	areite, -rei-	<*areite*>, <*-rei-*>
dipper	dita	<*dita*>
dish	dita	<*dita*>
deep basket	makuto	<*macuto*>
distance	ya-[1]	<*ya-*>
distance (near)	ai	<*ai-*>
distant	ya-[1]	<*ya-*>
do	ya-[2], yani	<*ya-*>, <*yani*>
doctor	behike, bohike, buhite, buhiti, bVhV-	<*behique*>, <*bohique*>, <*buhiti*>, <*buh(u)iti*>, <*bVhV-*>
dog	awõ, -wõ-[2]	<*aon*>, <*-on*>
don't	mayani	<*mayani*>
down	da-, dai-	<*da-*>, <*dai-*>
downward	daha-	<*daha-*>
drinking vessel	wawarei	<*guaguarei*>
drum	mawei, bayohabawo	<*maguey*>, < *baiohabao*>
dwelling	bo, bohi, buwi	<*bo*>, <*bohí-*>, <*buhuí*>
earring	tawawa	<*taguagua*>
earth	-uma, uku	<*-uma*>, <*ucu*>
east(ern)	hi-, i-[2]	<*hi-*>, <*i-*>
edge	ye-	<*ye-*>
end	maka, yarima	<*maca*>, <*yarima*>
enemy	anaki, -naki, makuri	<*anaqui*>, <*-naqui*>, <*macuri(x)*>
exchange	sera	<*serra*>
eye(s)	kako, -ako	<*caco*>, <*-ako*>
face	simu	<*zimu*>
far	ya[1]-	<*ya-*>
far(ther)	ai	<*ai-*>
farther	yaya	<*yaya-*>
farther back	waya-	<*guaya-*>
farthest	ayai-	<*ayai-*>
fire-fly	kokuyo	<*cocuyo*>
first	aba	<*aba*>
flower	ana	<*ana*>
foolish	sanako, siwato	<*sanaco*>, <*ciguato*>
foreign	maku-	<*maco/u-*>
foreigner	makuri	<*macuri(x)*>
foreland	aná, ané	<*aná*>, <*ané*>

Table 12. *Continued*

English	Taíno	Source spelling
forest	arabuko	<ar(c)abuco>
forest(ed)	bisa-, saba-	<biza->, <saba->
four	yamōkobre	<yamoncóbre>
free	wawa	<guagua>
friend	ku[1], tiyawo	<co/u>, <tiao>
frog	mako, mariwana, tona	<maco>, <mariguana>, <tona>
frontier	isi-, -kowa[1]	<isi->, <-coa>
furniture	tereke	<tereque>
generous	matū	<matum>
genipa	hawa	<xagua>
gentleman	matūheri, mekina, mikina	<matunheri>, <-mechina>, <-miquina>
gentleman	nitaino, bahari	<nitayno>, <bahari>
girdle	kairo	<cairo>
glass bead	kakona	<cacona>
god	semi	<zemí>
gold	kawōna, -wō-[1]	<caona>, <-on->
good	taino	<tayno>
grandfather	-roko-	<-roco->
grater	wayo	<guayo>
great	ba-	<ba->
greater	baha, baya-	<baha->, <baya->
greatest	bā-	<ban->
great man	bahari	<baharí>
group	lu-, yu-[1]	<lu->, <yu->
guanabana	wanabana	<guanábana>
guava	wayaba	<guayaba>
gulf	xama	<xama>
hammock	hamaka	<hamaca>
hammock ropes	hiko	<hico>
hard (in texture)	si-[1]	<ci->
have	-ka[3]	<-ca>
head	-si-[2]	<-c/si->
head chief	yō-	<yon->
headland	aná, ané, isi-	<aná>, <ané>, <isi->
headwaters	isi-	<isi->
hear	kama, kam-	<cama>
heaven(s)	turé	<turey>
height(s)	awu, wiho, yuya-	<abu>, <huiho>, <yuya->
high(er)	yu-[2]	<yu->
higher	yū-, yuya-	<yun->, <yuya->
highland(s)	awu, wiho, yuya-	<abu>, <huiho>, <yuya->
hills	iti-	<iti->
hinterland	kotu-	<cotu->
hole	we-	<hue->

Continued on the next page

Table 12. *Continued*

English	Taíno	Source spelling
home	**bo, bohi, buwi**	*‹bo›, ‹bohí-›, ‹buhuí›*
home people	**-bori**	*‹-borí›*
house	**bo, bohi, buwi**	*‹bo›, ‹bohí-›, ‹buhuí›*
house (rectangular)	**kané**	*‹caney›*
householders	**bohiyo**	*‹bohio›*
hurricane	**hurakā**	*‹huracán›*
hutía	**hutiya**	*‹hutía›*
I (am)	**daka**	*‹daca›*
iguana	**iwana**	*‹iguana›*
inlet (from the sea)	**xama**	*‹xama›*
interior	**maya-**	*‹-maya-›*
irritated	**sinato**	*‹cynato›*
island	**kaya, ke**	*‹caya›*
jewel	**yari**	*‹yari›*
junction	**ka-²**	*‹ca-›*
just to the rear	**wahana-**	*‹guahana-›*
kill	**-ka-⁴, -kana**	*‹-ca›, ‹caná›*
know (?)	**-ita**	*‹-ita›*
lake	**xara**	*‹xara-›*
land	**ke, mona, wa-, -wo**	*‹ke›, ‹mona›, ‹gua-›, ‹-wo›*
large	**ba-**	*‹ba-›*
large area of land	**-buko**	*‹-buco›*
large land	**kē**	*‹quen›*
larger	**baha, baya-**	*‹baha-›, ‹baya-›*
large rock outcrop	**bukara**	*‹búcara›*
largest	**bā-**	*‹ban-›*
leader	**tekina**	*‹tequina›*
leading	**yo-¹**	*‹yo-›*
leave	**-iba**	*‹-ibbá›*
less high	**yuna-**	*‹yuna-›*
less southerly	**waina-**	*‹guayna-›*
lesser foremost	**abana**	*‹abana›*
lesser of the upper	**haina**	*‹haina›*
lesser outside(rs)	**kubana**	*‹cubana›*
let us leave	**waiba**	*‹guaibbá›*
listen	**kama, kam-**	*‹cama›*
look	**-rikē**	*‹-riquen›*
louse	**hiriwawo**	*‹jiriguao›*
lower	**da-**	*‹da-›*
low grade of gold	**wanī**	*‹guanín›*
mainland	**kē**	*‹quen›*
maize	**mahisi**	*‹máhici›, ‹mahiz›*
male	**-he-, -xe-**	*‹-xe-›*
man	**-heri, bahari**	*‹-xeri›*
manatee	**manati**	*‹manatí›*

Table 12. *Continued*

English	Taíno	Source spelling
manioc	yuka	<*yuca*>
manioc juice	hiyē	<*hyen*>
mask	waisa	<*guaiza*>
master	tekina	<*tequina*>
meeting place	ka-², kawa	<*ca-*>, <*cagua*>
middle	ma-	<*ma-*>
middle (of a place)	nakā	<*nacan*>
middle folk	mari-	<*marí-*>
middle side	maha	<*maha*>
midmost	mā-	<*man-*>
midsection	maha	<*maha*>
midwestern	maya-	<*-maya-*>
mosquito	maye	<*maye*>
mountainous	wiho	<*huiho*>
mountain range	ruku-	<*rucu-*>
much	teketa	<*techeta*>
native people	-bori	<*-borí*>
natural sink-hole	xawe(i)	<*xague(y)*>
near	hi-, i-²	<*hi-*>, <*i-*>
net	nasa	<*nasa*>
northerly (most)	kā-, kahai-, hai-	<*cahai-*>, <*can-*>, <*hai-*>
northern	ka-¹, kai-, ha-	<*ca-*>, <*cai-*>, <*ha-*>
northernmost	kā-, kahai-	<*cahai-*>, <*can-*>
northern people	kayu	<*cayu*>
ocean	bawa, wā-	<*bagua*>, <*gua-*>
one	heketi	<*hequetí*>
ornament	yari	<*yari*>
out(er)	-ko	<*-co*>
out-country	-kowa¹	<*-coa*>
outside(rs)	kuba	<*cuba*>
paddle	nahe	<*nahe*>
papaya	papaya	<*papaya*>
paramount chief	yō-	<*yon-*>
parrot	hiwaka	<*higuaca*>
peanut	kakawete, -kawe-, mani	<*cacahuete*>, <*-cague-*>, <*maní*>
people	lu-, yu-¹	<*lu-*>, <*yu-*>
pineapple	yayawa	<*yayagua*>
plantation	kōnuko	<*conuco*>
planting (crops)	kō-	<*con-*>
planting stick	kowa²	<*coa*>
pond	xa-	<*xa-*>
pool	xa-	<*xa-*>
place	bo, bohi, buwi, wa-	<*bo*>, <*bohí-*>, <*buhuí*>, <*gua-*>
plaza	baté	<*batey*>
prince	mabo	<*mabó*>

Continued on the next page

Table 12. *Continued*

English	Taíno	Source spelling
princeling	mabona	<*mabona*>
rear	waha-	<*guaha-*>
rear-most	wãi-	<*guani-*>
red pepper	ahi[1]	<*axi*>
remora (fish)	waikan	<*guaicán*>
reward	kakona	<*cacona*>
ridge	ruku-	<*rucu-*>
river	bõ, mõ, -ri-	<*bõ*>, <*mõ*>, <*-ri-*>
river (?)	ari(ke)	<*ari(que)*>
river-grass	i[1]	<*y*>
rocky place	sibawo	<*sibao*>
rope	kabuya, -buya	<*cabuya*>, <*-buya*>
rough	si-[1]	<*ci-*>
saltwater	wã-	<*gua-*>
sand	si-[1]	<*ci-*>
sandal	kotara	<*cotara*>
savage(s)	bi-	< *bi-*>
savages (many)	bibi-	<*bibi-*>
savannah	sabana	<*sabana*>
sea	bawa, wa-	<*bagua*>, <*gua-*>
sea snail	siwa	<*cigua*>
second(ary)	yabã-, yamõ-	<*yaban-*> <*yamon-*>
see	-rikẽ	<*-riquen*>
shaman	behike, bohike, buhite, buhiti, bVhV-	<*behique*>, <*bohique*>, <*buhiti*>,<*buh(u)iti*>, <*bVhV-*>
shelter	bo, bohi, buwi	<*bo*>, <*bohí-*>, <*buhuí*>
shore	-kowa[1]	<*-coa*>
single	heketi	<*hequetí*>
sir	matũheri, mekina, mikina, nitaino, bahari	<*matunheri*>, <*-mechina*>, <*-miquina*>, <*nitayno*>, <*bahari*>
skin	-ura, kara	<*-ra*>, <*cara*>
sky	turé	<*turey*>
small canoe	kayuko, -yuko	<*cayuco*>, <*-yuco*>
smaller rodent	mohi	<*mohí*>
small sea turtle	hikoteya	<*hicotea*>
small meeting place	kawana	<*caguana-*>
snail	kowo	<*cobo*>
soil	uku	<*ucu*>
song	areite, -rei-	<*areite*>, <*-rei-*>
sound (= bay)	xama	<*xama*>
southerly	da-, dai-	<*da-*>, <*dai-*>
southern	wai-	<*guai-*>
southward	daha-	<*daha-*>
speak	-hiya, ahiyaka	<*-hiya*>, <*ahiyaca*>
species of rodent	kemi	<*quemí*>

Table 12. *Continued*

English	Taíno	Source spelling
species of rodent	kuri	<*curí*>
specter	hupiya	<*hupía*>
spirit of the dead	opiya, operito	<*opía*>, <*operito*>
Spondias sp	hobo	<*hobo*>
sticky	neibowa	<*neiboa*>
stone	siba	<*ziba*>
stone knife	manaya	<*manaya*>
strange	maku-	<*maco/u-*>
stupid	sanako, siwato	<*sanaco*>, <*ciguato*>
sunset	asu	<*asu*>
sunset	-su	<*-su*>
supernatural spirit	semi	<*zemí*>
swamp(y)	-misi	<*-misi*>
sweet potato	hahe	<*hage*>
tambourine	bayohabawo	<*baiohabao*>
temple	ku^2	<*cu*>
terminus	maka	<*maca*>
termite	komehẽ	<*comejen*>
terrain	uku	<*ucu*>
three	kanokū	<*canocúm*>
tobacco	tabako	<*tabaco*>
tobacco powder	kohowa	<*cohoba*>
tooth	ahi^2	<*-ahi-*>
toothless	mahite	<*mahite*>
top	ka-^{1}, kai-	<*ca-*>, <*cai-*>
topmost	kā-, kahai-	<*cahai-*>, <*can-*>
topward	kaiya-	<*caya-*>
toward	-yo^2	<*-yo*>
trade	sera	<*serra*>
tree	ara	<*ara*>
trees (small)	karabuco	<*carabuco*>
tribe	lu-, yu-^{1}	<*lu-*>, <*yu-*>
trough	bateya	<*batea*>
two	yamoka	<*yamocá*>
type of palm	yawa	<*yagua*>
type of small shark	haketa	<*haqueta*>
undergrowth	maniwa, tabuko	<*maigua*>, <*tabuco*>
unfriendly	maku-	<*maco/u-*>
unsettled	bisa-	<*bisa-*>
up(per)	hai-	<*hai-*>
upland	iti-	<*iti-*>
upper	ha-	<*ha-*>
uppermost	hã-, kā-	<*han-*>, <*can*>
upstream	kasa-	<*casa-*>
utensil	tereke	<*tereque*>

Continued on the next page

Table 12. *Continued*

English	Taíno	Source spelling
valley	**itku-**	*<itcu->*
village	**inkayeke**	*<incaieque>*
vine	**behuko**	*<bejuco>*
water	**xa-, -ne, -ni**	*<-ne>, <-ni>*
weakness in the legs	**wawana**	*<guaguana>*
weeds	**karabuco**	*<carabuco>*
western	**ai, asu, -su, ya[1]-**	*<ay->, <asu>, <-su>, <ya->*
westernmost	**ayai-**	*<ayai->*
woman's loin-cloth	**nawa**	*<nagua>*
wood	**ara, sa-** (?)	*<ara>, <sa->*
wooden bowl	**wariketē**	*<guariquetén>*
wooden club	**makana**	*<macana>*
woods	**arabuko**	*<ar(c)abuco>*
work	**-bori**	*<-bori->*
work(er)	**-boriya**	*<-boría>*

11

Antillean Languages
An Afterview

In the previous ten chapters we have attempted to describe the pre-Columbian languages of the Greater and Lesser Antilles as seen through the surviving data, providing examples of the lesser known ones—Ciguayo, Macorís, Guanahatabey, and, particularly, Taíno—and referring the interested reader to additional materials on Lesser Antillean Eyeri/Island Carib/Kalíphuna/Garífuna and the Carib Karina language. We have also presented what we feel are the most important findings of archaeological work in the islands through 2001 as they relate to things-linguistic, and have, in Chapter 1 and the References section, referred the reader to additional sources on the reconstruction of Antillean prehistory. We have used the language data not as language data per se, but, as we have shown, as a comparative tool to determine if the combination of linguistic and archaeological data might lead us toward a hypothesis concerning the origins and movements of the Antillean peoples. Some in the fields of linguistics and archaeology may not agree with our suggestions or conclusions, but the hypothesis is one which needs, and could readily have, further testing. Future researchers will perhaps flesh it out, adding what needs to be added, pruning where pruning may be called for, and refining the process of clarification.

At the time of Spanish intervention there were seven different speech communities in the Antilles: (1) *Ciboney Taíno* in Hispaniola (central and southern Haiti), all of central Cuba, all but the southern Lucayan Islands, and Jamaica; (2) *Macorís,* in two dialects, in the Dominican Republic section of northern Hispaniola; (3) *Ciguayo* on the Samaná Peninsula of northeastern Hispaniola; (4) *Guanahatabey* in Pinar del Río province of far eastern Cuba; (5) *Classic Taíno* in Hispaniola (primarily the section which is now the Dominican Republic), Puerto Rico, Vieques and the Virgin Islands, and in the Leeward Islands; (6) *Kalíphuna* in the Windward Islands; and (7) *Karina Carib* in the Windwards.

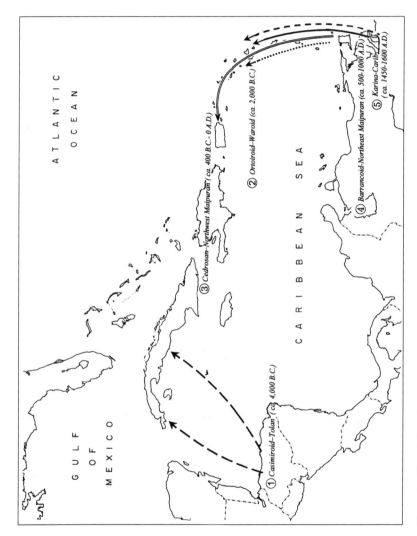

Fig. 8. Antillean Migrations

Our reconstruction of events in the pre-Columbian Antilles, graphically shown on the map in Figure 8, encompasses five major physical migrations of peoples into the islands, commencing about 4000 B.C. and completing themselves about the year 1500–1600 A.D. Two additional migrations mentioned later in the chapter—a Huecan and a Meillacan—may have taken place, but, while archaeological and linguistic data tell us that something quite unusual was going on, we are not at all sure of the nature of the phenomena in question nor of the fact that the phenomena were caused by migrations of outside peoples. The five certain and two possible migrations are what might be called *External Migrations,* inasmuch as the peoples involved originated outside the Antillean region and brought their new cultures into an arena in which they had not earlier been found. There were also what can be called *Internal Migrations* within the islands, involving the spread of peoples and cultures already there from their homelands into other parts of the Antilles. In this afterview of the data and its implications each type of migration will be handled separately. References and substantiating data will be found in the individual earlier chapters and have purposely not been repeated here in order to present a perhaps more concise, clearer view of Antillean linguistic prehistory.

EXTERNAL MIGRATIONS

The First Migration (ca. 4000 B.C.)

Both archaeological and linguistic data lead us to believe that the first migration into the Antilles came prior to 4000 B.C., when the people ancestral to the Ciguayo, migrating from the coast of Belize-Honduras, discovered and settled the then uninhabited Greater Antilles. The Ciguayo language of 1492 was a language whose closest parallels are with the Tolan languages of the Honduran coast of Central America, and glottochronological data suggest a separation of ancestral Ciguayo from the Tolan mainstream in Central America well before 3000 B.C. The language data we have indicate a Ciguayo presence only on Hispaniola in 1492, but archaeological data indicate an earlier presence in Cuba and Puerto Rico as well, with a probable presence in the Leeward Islands of the northern Lesser Antilles. Archaeologically defined as the Casimiroid Tradition, their limited numbers and isolated geographical location at the time of European contact—inhabiting only the Samaná Peninsula of far northeastern Hispaniola—indicates a remnant population of a once larger and more widespread group, forced into its 1492 geographical cul-de-sac by pressure from later more dominant groups entering the region from the south and east and pushing northward and westward through the Greater Antilles.

The Casimiroid people represented a Lithic tradition—they were makers and users of stone tools—and subsisted on food resources naturally available to them. Unlike later peoples of the Antilles, they did not make or use pottery nor practice agriculture. While it is unlikely that additional Ciguayo language data will turn up, archaeological work in Ciguayo territory may well help clarify the cultural relationships of this shadowy people to the other Greater Antillean ethnic groups through a careful characterization of the types of tools they used, their methods and materials of manufacture, and the nature of the settlements in which the Ciguayo lived.

The Second Migration (ca. 2000 B.C.)

At some time around 2000 B.C. a new people entered the Antilles. Like the Casimiroids, they represent a lithic tradition, though modified by the use of tools of bone and shell as well—such cultures are referred to as Archaic cultures. They, too, were non-agricultural and were not pottery-makers. The origin of these newcomers has not been firmly established by archaeological research, for they occur only in the Greater Antilles and the Leeward Islands, at the northern end of the Lesser Antilles. Convincingly similar sites are found only sporadically in the intervening Windward Islands, at the southern end of the Lesser Antilles. Language data from the Greater Antilles—both Cuba and Hispaniola—offer a solution, however, for the presence of a language related to the Warao languages of the northern coast of Venezuela and the Orinoco Delta is indicated in Cuba, Hispaniola, and, possibly, Puerto Rico. A Warao-like language could hardly have gotten to the Greater Antilles any way but up from Venezuela through the Lesser Antilles, and the seeming data-gap in the Windward Islands is likely the result of the fact that so little archaeological work has yet been done in the Windwards.

The early Warao peoples of Venezuela are referred to as Waroid, because it is probable that a number of closely Warao-related languages were spoken along the long Venezuelan coastline from Lake Maracaibo eastward to the Orinoco Delta in pre-Columbian times. Their Archaic Age cultures at the 2000 B.C. time-level are called Ortoiroid, and the Archaic Age archaeological sites in the Leeward Islands and the Greater Antilles are Ortoiroid in nature. Thus, the origin of this second migration into the Antilles was most probably the Orinoco Delta and coastal Venezuela, and the language of the people was likely Waroid. All of the surviving language data from the Greater Antilles for the pre-Taíno people, except two Ciguayo words, is Waroid in nature and is limited to those peoples whom the Taíno called *Macorís,* which means 'The Foreigners' in Taíno.

Like the Ciguayo, the Macorís people had been pushed back toward the north coast of Hispaniola and the sea by the later Taíno migration. Their conquest by the Taíno and their conversion to Arawak ways was still in progress when the Spanish arrived in 1492. In some parts of Hispaniola and Cuba the contact resulted in a creolized people and language referred to as Ciboney Taíno, discussed subsequently under the heading of Internal Migrations.

The Third Migration (400 B.C.–1 A.D.)

Around 400 to 200 B.C. a third people, destined to form the islands' major ethnic group, began to move northward from Trinidad into the Antilles. These were the people ancestral to the natives first encountered by Columbus when he landed on Guanahaní island in the Lucayan chain on October 12, 1492. They came to call themselves Taíno, which translates as 'The Good Ones' or 'The Good People' (*taí-* 'good' + -*no* 'a pluralizing suffix'). The Good People, between 400 B.C. and the time of the birth of Christ, penetrated every island in the Antilles chain from Trinidad to central Cuba. The only region they had not yet conquered by the time of the arrival of the Europeans was far western Cuba, which remained in the hands of the Guanahatabey people, probable descendants of some of the last Ortoiroid, Macorís-speaking people in the islands.

From our language data we know with certainty that the Taíno spoke a Northwest Maipuran Arawakan language, distantly related to that of their Goajiro kinsmen still living to the west of Lake Maracaibo on the coast of western Venezuela and northeastern Colombia. We know that archaeologically their pottery-making, agricultural tradition had its genesis in the region where the Apuré and Orinoco Rivers come together in west-central Venezuela. The cultural tradition of these people, going back as early as 2000 B.C. with their Ronquinian ancestors, is called Saladoid, and the particular branch of the Saladoid people who moved into the Antilles from the island of Trinidad are called the Cedrosan Saladoid people after the Cedros site on Trinidad.

Beginning about 400 B.C., the Cedrosan people moved rapidly through the archipelago from Trinidad to the Mona Passage area separating Puerto Rico and Hispaniola, reaching there by the time of the birth of Christ. Interestingly, the earliest Cedrosan Saladoid sites in the Antilles are found in the Leeward Islands rather than in the more southerly Windward Islands, but since we know for certain that the source of both the Saladoid Tradition and of the Taíno language lay in Venezuela, it seems quite certain that the lack of early Cedrosan Windward sites is simply a reflection of our imperfect knowledge of the archaeology of those islands. We do know that most Cedrosan sites occur on the higher islands and that they are usually located away from the sea, preferably upriver from the seashore, and near heavily forested, jungled areas. This contrasts strongly with the Ortoiroid preference for the lower-lying islands and settlement right on the shore.

The Cedrosan people, then, brought with them not only a pottery-making, agricultural tradition, but also a Northwest Maipuran language. With the rapid expansion of the Cedrosan people, their language, which we call pre-Taíno, soon became the dominant language of the entire Antilles. Certainly from 1 A.D. until about 500 A.D. Taíno was the language of the realm and a *lingua franca* understood and used by all throughout both the Greater and Lesser Antilles, regardless of their native tongue.

The Fourth Migration (500–1000 A.D.)

About 500 A.D. a second Arawak-speaking people, the Barrancoid people, pottery-makers and agriculturists like the Cedrosans, entered the islands from the Orinoco Delta and Trinidad. Their origins lay, about 2100 B.C., in the middle Orinoco Valley, considerably to the east of the ancestral Saladoid peoples. By the early years of the Christian era they had replaced the Saladoid peoples of the Delta and Trinidad and begun to move into the Windward Islands. The trademark of their culture is their technically sophisticated, highly decorated ceramic wares, which begin to appear in otherwise Cedrosan sites in the Windwards by 500 A.D. There is every indication that the Barrancoid people first entered the Antilles as traders, for they were known throughout the Orinoco region as the area's paramount merchants, to judge from archaeological evidence. The fact that Cedrosan culture is not replaced in the Windwards, but, rather, simply augmented by Barrancoid pottery, also points to this conclusion rather than outright settlement in any great numbers.

By the middle 600s, however, there must have been genuine Barrancoid colonies of some size throughout the Windward Islands, for a new ceramic tradition, referred to as the Troumassoid Tradition, appears, a blend of the Cedrosan and Barrancoid past. During the next 500 years, as revealed archaeologically, this blend of cultural characteristics became a true fusion, and by 1000 A.D. a new creolized culture, the Suazoid, which lasted until the mid-1400s, emerged.

It is of considerable interest and importance to note that Barrancoid, Troumassoid, and Suazoid potteries do not occur north of Guadeloupe, the northernmost of the Windward Islands. Though some Barrancoid influence is reflected in the ceramics and other artifactual types of the Leeward Islands, the Virgin Islands, and neighboring Vieques and eastern Puerto Rico, there is no evidence that those areas were settled by Barrancoid people. The Barrancoid settlers and their cultural successors were geographically restricted to the Windward Islands.

These geographical limits seem to have been imposed by linguistic constraints, for it is clear from documentary evidence left by Columbus and the Spanish chroniclers that the people of the Windward Islands spoke a language other than Taíno. The people called themselves *Eyeri* (sometimes written as Iñeri or Igneri), which means 'The Men' or 'The People' in the sense of 'Human

Beings,' and though the Spanish had little contact with them, they are noted in the earliest Spanish writings—letters from crewmen on Columbus's second voyage in 1493—as being quite different in appearance, behavior, and language from the inhabitants of the Greater Antilles. All of this evidence, archaeological and historical, implies the presence of a new Arawakan language in the Windward Islands, one which by Suazoid times had replaced Taíno as the language commonly spoken there.

We are fortunate that the descendant of the Eyeri language, Garífuna, is still spoken today, and we have clear historical documentation that the ancestors of the 75,000-some Garífuna people now living in Belize, Guatemala, and Honduras were, indeed, the Eyeri. Modern Garífuna was called Kalíphuna when it was first recorded in detail by the French priest Fr. Raymond Breton, and its speakers then told the French that the language was that of their ancestors. Analysis of both Garífuna and its seventeenth-century form, Kalíphuna, indicates that the language belongs to the Northeast Maipuran group within the Arawakan language family, the same group to which the modern Lokono language of the Guianas belongs.

The Arawakan languages of the middle Orinoco River Valley today are still Northeast Maipuran, and it is thus most probable that the language of the Barrancoid people belonged to the same Maipuran subgroup. Inasmuch as Taíno, though Arawakan, belongs to the more distantly related Northwest Maipuran languages, like Goajiro, Eyeri and its descendants would have been largely unintelligible to Taíno speakers—in somewhat the same relationship that modern Spanish has to modern Portuguese. Thus the Barrancoid people were probably responsible for the replacement of Northwest Maipuran Taíno by Northeast Maipuran Eyeri in the Windward Islands, just as they were responsible for the replacement of Cedrosan Saladoid artifactual traits by Barrancoid traits. The full amalgamation of the two cultures—Windward Islands Cedrosan pre-Taíno and Barrancoid to form the new, Eyeri culture seems to have reached its full fruition with the Suazoid people, between 1000 and 1450 A.D.

The Fifth Migration (1450–ca. 1600)

Sometime during the middle of the fifteenth century, to judge from radiocarbon dates, the Eyeri people stopped making Suazoid ceramic wares. Archaeologically little is known of the post-1400 prehistory of the Windward Islands, but we have Spanish accounts from 1493 and, sporadically, throughout the following century which indicate the presence of a people quite different from the Taíno people of the Greater Antilles and the Leeward Islands. We now know, as pointed out above, that their language was Arawakan, descended from the Eyeri of a century before. We also know, from French documentation from 1635 and the following decades, that the inhabitants of the Windward Islands no longer called themselves Eyeri but, rather, *Kalínago* or *Kalíphuna*. The men used the first term, which means 'The Honorable Manioc People' (*kali*'manioc' + -*na* 'a pluralizing suffix' + -*go* 'an honorific suffix'). The second term, used by the women, means 'Members of the Manioc Clan' (*kali* 'manioc' + -*phu* 'clan' + -*na* 'a pluralizing suffix'). The Kalíphuna, as we have called them in this book—for their twenty-first-century descendants in the Windward Islands still refer to themselves as *Karifuna*—told the French that their origins were partly there in the islands, but that they were also on the South American mainland with the *Karina*, a Carib people of the Guianas—again, Karina means 'The Manioc People' (*kari* 'manioc' + -*na* 'a pluralizing suffix'). The Karina men had come on raiding and trading expeditions to the islands beginning some 200 years earlier, according to island oral tradition, had taken Eyeri wives, and had stayed, newcomers arriving in increasing numbers over the years.

The Kalíphuna had, in other words, become a creolized people of mixed Arawakan Eyeri and Carib Karina ancestry. The creolization was evident in the language, which was still grammatically largely Eyeri Arawak but with approximately 11 percent of its vocabulary taken from the Carib Karina language, and 56 percent of its vocabulary embracing Karina words which only the men used and the same percentage of Eyeri words used for the same concepts and things by the women. The nature of Eyeri artifacts became altered as well, and we find new ceramic wares, called Cayo wares on St. Vincent, quite unrelated to the earlier Barrancoid Troumassoid–Suazoid tradition.

The fifth and last migration into the Antilles was, in summary, that of the Karina Carib people from the Guianas, who, beginning about 1450 A.D. came, intermarried with the Eyeri and over the years gave rise to what came to be known as the Island Carib people, part Carib, part Eyeri Arawak. Historical records indicate that Karina-speakers continued to come into the lower Windward Islands, particularly Grenada, at least as late as the 1650s.

Possible Additional External Migrations

A possible sixth external migration during Cedrosan Saladoid times, about 150 B.C., has been suggested as an explanation for the unique artifactual traits found in the Sorcé and Punta Candelero sites on Vieques and southeast Puerto Rico. Its sources are postulated to be the Río Guapo ceramic styles of the central Venezuelan coast.

There may also have been yet a seventh external migration of Eastern Maipuran Arawakan speakers directly from the Guianas to the northern coast of Hispaniola, for both north Hispaniolan Macorís and Lucayan Ciboney Taíno show lexical influence from some non-Taíno, non-Eyeri Maipuran Arawakan language in the forms *baésa* (Hispaniolan Macorís) and *Bímini* and *Lukayunéke* (Lucayan Ciboney Taíno). It was been suggested that such a migration came from the southern Guiana coast sometime around the early 700 A.D. period, giving rise to the Meillacan style of Ostionoid pottery, but so far there is no external evidence to support or refute this suggestion. The data on both possible migrations, Huecan and Meillacan, are at present inconclusive, and both possible migrations demand considerably more archaeological investigation before any definite conclusions can be reached.

INTERNAL MIGRATIONS

The internal migrations of people within the Antilles are not as easy to define and describe as the external migrations which brought new populations to the islands. They are so far, in fact, impossible to define for the Windward Islands, simply because so little archaeological work has yet been done in those islands. We are more fortunate in our attempts to reconstruct the internal movements of peoples in the Greater Antilles, their Lucayan outliers, and the Leeward Islands, since we have a considerable amount of both archaeological and linguistic data on which to base our conclusions. These conclusions have been one of the main focuses of this book, and, rather than repeat the details, they may be summarized as follows.

Ciguayo, a Central American Tolan language originally spoken throughout Cuba, Hispaniola, and probably Puerto Rico, if their equation with the Casimiroid Tradition is correct, was moribund in 1492 and extinct very shortly thereafter. The peripheral position of Ciguayo in 1492 may indicate that the Ortoiroid, Waroid-speaking population which entered the region around 2000 B.C., while perhaps mixing with the older Casimiroid Tolan population, also forced at least some of the earlier Tolan speakers into less hospitable regions of the Greater Antilles. Toponymic evidence indicates that the Waroid language replaced the Tolan language throughout Hispaniola and Cuba except in the area occupied by the ethnohistoric Ciguayo.

All of the Greater Antillean language groups except Ciguayo show influence from a Waroid language. These parallels are lexical in Classic Taíno (*duho*) and Ciboney Taíno (*nosái*), toponymic in both Macorís and Guanahatabey. This language data would seem to indicate both the presence of Waroid language speakers in the Greater Antilles and their gradual displacement after about the first century A.D. by Taíno speakers. The shadowy Guanahatabey of far western Cuba fit the same geographical pattern, and, to judge from toponymic evidence, were possibly a remnant Waroid population forced into its geographical location by the movement of the more dominant pre-Taíno people from the east. From toponymic and ethnohistoric evidence the Waroid language seems to have survived only in far western Cuba (the Guanahatabey) and in north coastal Hispaniola (Upper and Lower Macorís).

The movements of the Taíno people on Hispaniola, ever expanding north-ward and westward from their Puerto Rican point of entry, caused either con-siderable population displacement or at least the whole-scale development of hybrid populations, part Taíno and part Ortoiroid and/or Casimiroid. The Taíno language gradually replaced the Waroid language in Puerto Rico and in eastern and central Hispaniola. In western Hispaniola and Cuba, however, it blended with the Waroid language to form a creolized idiom identified as the Ciboney dialect of Taíno. This dialect was largely Taíno in grammar and lexi-con, but retained some Waroid vocabulary. The creolization process accom-plished itself during the period between 400 and 900 A.D., accompanying the western expansion of Ostionan and early Meillacan ceramic wares. Both people and their accompanying Ciboney Taíno dialect and Meillacan artifactual traits spread to the Lucayan islands toward the middle of this period (Berman and Gnivecki 1991, 1995).

Classic Taíno became a *lingua franca* for all the Greater Antilles except the Guanahatabey region of Cuba, which, from archaeological evidence, the Taíno never penetrated. It also spread to the Turks and Caicos around 1200 A.D. with the migrations of the Classic Taíno–speaking people to those islands. This is evidenced by the presence of Chican ceramic wares in sites in that region and by historical tradition. About 1450 Classic Taíno also spread across Cabo Maisí from the northwestern peninsula of Haiti to what is now Oriente Province in far eastern Cuba. The latter migration was hastened and intensified by the ar-rival of the Spanish in 1492.

This is a summary picture of the pre-Columbian Antilles as seen from a combination of the language, archaeological, and ethnohistoric data discussed in the earlier chapters. Is it the final view? Without doubt it is not. The juxta-position of interrelated linguistic and archaeological data has, however, high-lighted topics eminently worthy of further investigation and resolution, which it is to be hoped the younger generations of pre-Columbian scholars, both ar-chaeologists and linguists, and those who come after them may address and resolve.

References

Academía Real de La Historia
1951   *Mapas Españoles de América, Siglos XV–XVII.* Edited by Duque de Alba. N.p., Madrid.

Alegría, Ricardo E.
1978   *Apuntes en Torno a la Mitología de los Indios Taínos de las Antillas Mayores y sus Orígenes Suramericanos.* Centro de Estudios Avanzados de Puerto Rico y el Caribe, San Juan.

1981   *El Uso de la Terminología Etno-Histórica para designar las Culturas Aborígenes de las Antillas.* Seminario de Historia de América, Universidad de Valladolid, Valladolid.

1983   *Ball Courts and Ceremonial Plazas in the West Indies. Yale University Publications in Anthropology No. 79.* Yale University Press, New Haven.

1993   *Índice Analítico de las Actas de los Congresos de la Asociación de Arqueología del Caribe, 1965–1993.* Centro de Estudios Avanzados de Puerto Rico y el Caribe, San Juan.

1997   The Study of Aboriginal Peoples: Multiple Ways of Knowing. In *The Indigenous People of the Caribbean,* edited by Samuel M. Wilson, pp. 9–19. University Press of Florida, Gainesville.

Allaire, Louis
1977   *Later Prehistory in Martinique and the Island Caribs: Problems in Ethnic Identification.* University Microfilms International, Ann Arbor.

1980   On the Historicity of Carib Migrations in the Lesser Antilles. *American Antiquity* 45:238–245.

1987   Some Comments of the Ethnic Identity of the Taino-Carib Frontier. In *Ethnicity and Culture,* edited by Reginald Auger et al., pp. 127–133. Archaeological Association, University of Calgary, Calgary.

1990   Prehistoric Taino Interaction with the Lesser Antilles: The View from Martinique, F. W. I. Paper presented at the 55th Annual Meeting of the Society For American Archaeology, Las Vegas, April 18, 1990.

1991   Understanding Suazy. In *Proceedings of the Thirteenth International Congress for*

Caribbean Archaeology, Held in Willemstad, Curaçao, On July 24–29, 1989, pp. 715–728. Archaeological-Anthropological Institute of the Netherlands Antilles, Willemstad.

1997a   The Lesser Antilles before Columbus. In *The Indigenous People of the Caribbean*, edited by Samuel M. Wilson, pp. 20–28. University Press of Florida, Gainesville.

1997b   The Caribs of the Lesser Antilles. In *The Indigenous People of the Caribbean*, edited by Samuel M. Wilson, pp. 179–185. University Press of Florida, Gainesville.

Allaire, Louis, and Mario Mattioni

1983   Boutbois et le Goudinot: Deux Gisements Acéramiques de La Martinique. In *Proceedings of the Ninth International Congress for the Study of Pre-Columbian Cultures of the Lesser Antilles, Held in the Dominican Republic, August 2–8, 1981*, pp. 27–38. Centre de Recherches Caraïbes, University of Montreal, Montreal.

Anghiera, Pietro Martire D' (Peter Martyr)

1892   *Fuentes Históricas sober Colón y América (Pedro Mártir de Anglería).* [1530] 4 Vols. Madrid.

Arrom, José Juan

1974   *Relación Acerca de las Antigüedades de los Indios: El Primer Tratado Escrito en América (Nueva Versión, Con Notas, Mapa y appendices).* Siglo XXI Editores, S.A., México.

1975   *Mitología y Arts Prehispánicas de las Antillas.* Siglo XXI Editores, S.A., México.

1990   La Lingual de Los Taínos: Aortas Lingüístico al Conocimiento de su Cosmovisión. In *La Cultural Tania*, pp. 53–64. Turner, Madrid.

Bahamas Archaeological Team

1984   *Archaeology in the Bahamas: Report for 1982/3.* Bahamas Archaeological Team, Nassau.

Berman, Mary Jane, and Perry L. Gnivecki

1991   The Colonization of the Bahamas Archipelago: A View from the Three Dog Site, San Salvador Island. *Proceedings of the Fourteenth International Congress for Caribbean Archaeology*, edited by A. Cummins and P. King, pp. 170–186. International Association for Caribbean Archaeology, Barbados.

1995   The Colonization of the Bahama Archipelago: A Reappraisal. *World Archaeology* 26(3):421–441.

Bernáldez, Andres

1930   *Historia de los Reyes Catholics. The Voyages of Christopher Columbus, Being the Journals of his First and Third, and the Letters concerning his First and Last Voyages, to which is now Added the Account of his Second Voyage, written by Andres Fernandez, Now Newly Translated and edited, with an Introduction and Notes by Cecil Jane.* London.

Biet, Antoine

1664   Voyage de la France Equinoxiale en l'Isle de Cayenne. In *Chez François Clouzier*, pp. 393–432. Paris.

Boomert, Aad

1985   The Cayo Complex of St. Vincent and Its Mainland Origin. Paper presented at the 11th International Congress for Caribbean Archaeology, San Juan.

1986   The Cayo Complex of St. Vincent: Ethnohistorical and Archaeological Aspects of the Island-Carib Problem. *Antropológica* (Caracas) 66:3–68.

Boucher, Philip P.

1992   *Cannibal Encounters: Europeans and Island Caribs, 1492–1763.* Johns Hopkins University Press, Baltimore.

Breton, Raymond

1647   *Relations de l'Ile de la Guadeloupe.* Reprinted 1978, Société d'Histoire de La Guadeloupe, Basse-Terre.

1665   *Dictionnaire Caraïbe-François.* Auxerre. Facsimile ed., 1900, Jules Platzmann, Leipzig.

1666   *Dictionnaire François-Caraïbe.* Auxerre. Facsimile ed., 1900, Jules Platzmann, Leipzig.

1667   *Grammaire Caraïbe.* Auxerre. New Ed. 1877, L. Adam & Ch. Leclerc, Paris.

Broadbent, Sylvia

1957   Rumsen I: Methods of Reconstitution. *International Journal of American Linguistics* 23:275–280.

Bullen, Ripley P.

1964   The Archaeology of Grenada, West Indies. *Contributions of the Florida State Museum, Social Sciences 11.* Florida State Museum, Gainesville.

Burch, Ernest A., Jr.

1975   *Eskimo Kinsmen.* American Ethnographical Society Monographs 59. West Publishing Co., St. Paul.

Campbell, Lyle

1979   Middle American Languages. In *The Languages of Native America,* edited by Lyle Campbell and Marianne Mithun, pp. 902–1000. University of Texas Press, Austin.

Chanca, Diego Álvarez

1949   *Navegaciones Colombinas.* Edited by Edmundo O'Gorman. Secretaria de Educación Pública, Mexico City.

Chanlatte Baik, Luis A.

1981   *La Hueca y Sorcé (Vieques, Puerto Rico): Primeras Migraciones Agroalfareras Antillanas (Nuevo Esquema para los Procesos Culturales de la Arqueología Antillana.* Privately printed, Santo Domingo.

1983   *Catálogo Arqueología de Vieques: Exposición del 13 de Marzo al 22 de Abril de 1983.* Museo de Antropología, Historia y Arte, University of Puerto Rico, Río Piedras.

Coe, William R.

1957   A Distinctive Artifact Common to Haiti and Central America. *American Antiquity* 22(3):280–282.

Colección de Documentos Inéditos

1864–86   *Colección de Documentos Inéditos Relativos al Descubrimiento, Conquista y Colonización de las Posesiones Españolas en América y Oceánia, sacados, en su mayor parte, del Real Archivo de Indias.* Bajo la Dirección de D./ Joaquín F. Pacheco y Don Francisco de Cárdenas, Miembros de Varias Reales Academias Científicas; y de D. Luís Torres de Mendoza . . . Imprenta de Manuel B. de Quirós, Madrid.

Columbus, Christopher

1988   *Select Documents Illustrating the Four Voyages of Columbus.* Translated and edited by Cecil Jane. Dover, New York.

Conzemius, Édouard

1922   The Jicaques of Honduras. *International Journal of American Linguistics* 2:163–170.

Danielssen, Bengt

1949   Some Attraction and Repulsion Patterns among Jíbaro Indians. *Sociometry* 12:83–105.

Davis, Dave D.

1974   Some Notes Concerning the Archaic Occupation of Antigua. In *Proceedings of the Fifth International Congress for the Study of Pre-Columbian Cultures of the Lesser Antilles, Antigua, July 22–28, 1973*, pp. 65–71. Antigua Archaeological Society, St. Johns, Antigua.

Davis, Dave D., and R. Christopher Goodwin

1990   Island Carib Origins: Evidence and Nonevidence. *American Antiquity* 55(1):37–48.

De Booy, Theodoor

1912   Lucayan Remains in the Caicos Islands. *American Anthropologist,* New Series 14:81–105.

Deagan, Kathleen A.

1987   Initial Encounters: Arawak Responses to European Contact at En Bas Saline, Haiti. In *Columbus and his World: First San Salvador Conference,* pp. 341–359. College Center of the Finger Lakes, Bahamian Field Station, San Salvador, Bahamas.

De Goeje, C. H.

1939   Nouvelle Examen des langues des Antilles avec notes sur les langues Arawak-Maipuré et Caribe et vocabulaires Shebayo et Guayana (Guayane). *Journal de la Société des Américanistes de Paris* 31:1–120.

Delpuech, André

2001   Historical Archaeology in the French West Indies. In *Island Lives: Historical Archaeologies of the Caribbean,* edited by Paul Farnsworth, pp. 21–59. The University of Alabama Press, Tuscaloosa.

Dennis, Ronald K., and Margaret Royce Dennis

1983   *Diccionario Tol (Jicaque)-Español y Español-Tol (Jicaque).* Instituto Lingüístico de Verano en Colaboración con el Instituto Hondureño de Antropología e Historia, Tegucigalpa.

Du Tertre, J. B.

1667   *Histoire Générale des Antilles: Habitués par les François.* 4 vols. Th. Jolly, Paris. Reprinted 1978 by E. Kolodziej, Fort-de-France, Martinique.

Dyen, Isadore

1956   Language Distribution and Migration Theory. *Language* 32:611–626.

Evans, Clifford, and Betty J. Meggers

1960   *Archeological Investigations in British Guiana.* Bureau of American Ethnology Bulletin 177. Smithsonian Institution, Washington, D.C.

Ewen, Charles R.

2001   Historical Archaeology in the Colonial Spanish Caribbean. In *Island Lives: Historical Archaeology of the Caribbean,* edited by Paul Farnsworth, pp. 3–20. The University of Alabama Press, Tuscaloosa.

Farnsworth, Paul, editor

2001   *Island Lives: Historical Archaeologies of the Caribbean.* The University of Alabama Press, Tuscaloosa.

Febles, J., and A. V. Rives, editors

1991   *Arqueología de Cuba y de Otras Áreas Antillanas.* Centro de Antropología, Editorial Academia, La Habana.

Fewkes, Jesse W.

1904   The Prehistoric Culture of Cuba. *American Anthropologist,* New Series 6(5).

1907   The Aborigines of Porto Rico and Neighboring Islands. In *Annual Report of the Bureau of American Ethnology for 1903-04,* no. 25, pp. 1–220. Smithsonian Institution, Washington, D.C.

1922   *A Prehistoric Island Culture Area of America. Bureau of American Ethnology Annual Report 34 (For 1912–13),* pp. 35–281. Smithsonian Institution, Washington, D.C.

Figueredo, Alfredo

1976   Caño Hondo: Un Residuario Precerámico en la Isla de Vieques. *Proceedings of the Seventh International Congress for the Study of Pre-Columbian Cultures of the Lesser Antilles,* pp. 247–252. Centre de Recherches Caraïbes, Université de Montréal, Montreal.

1987   Brief Introduction to the Prehistory of St. Croix, from Earliest Times to 1493. Society of Virgin Island Historians *Bulletin* 1(1):4–10.

Fleming, Ilah, and Ronald K. Dennis

1977   Tol (Jicaque) Phonology. *International Journal of American Linguistics* 43:121–127.

Fuson, Robert H.

1987   *The Log of Christopher Columbus.* International Marine Publishing Company, Camden, Maine.

Gonzalez, Nancie L.

1988   *Sojourners of the Caribbean: Ethnogenesis and Ethnohistory of the Garífuna.* University of Illinois Press, Urbana.

1997   The Garifuna of Central America. In *The Indigenous People of the Caribbean,* edited by Samuel M. Wilson, pp. 197–205. University Press of Florida, Gainesville.

Goodwin, R. Christopher

1978   The Lesser Antilles Archaic: New Data from St. Kitts. *Journal of The Virgin Islands Archaeological Society* 5:6–16.

Granberry, Julian

1955   *A Survey of Bahamian Archeology.* M.A. Thesis, Department of Anthropology, University of Florida, Gainesville.

1956   The Cultural Position of the Bahamas in Caribbean Archaeology. *American Antiquity* 22(2):128–134.

1958 *An Archaeological Survey of the Cayman Islands.* Unpublished report and notes in possession of the author.

1978 The Gordon Hill Site, Crooked Island, Bahamas. *Journal of the Virgin Islands Archaeological Society* 6:32–44.

1991a Lucayan Toponyms. *Journal of the Bahamas Historical Society* 13(1):3–12.

1991b Was Ciguayo a West Indian Hokan Language? *International Journal of American Linguistics* 57(4):514–519.

Granberry, Julian, and John Winter

1995 Bahamian Ceramics. *Proceedings of The Fifteenth International Congress for Caribbean Archaeology,* pp. 3–15. Centro de Estudios Avanzados de Puerto Rico y el Caribe, con la Colaboración de la Fundación Puertorriqueña de las Humanidades y la Universidad de Puerto Rico, San Juan.

Greenberg, Joseph

1960 General Classification of Central and South American Languages. In *Men and Culture: Selected Papers,* edited by Anthony F. C. Wallace, pp. 791–794. Fifth International Congress of Anthropological and Ethnological Sciences, September 1–9, 1956. University of Pennsylvania Press, Philadelphia.

Gross, Jeffrey Martin

1976 The Archaic Period of the Virgin Islands: New Evidence and Investigations. *Proceedings of the Sixth International Congress for the Study of Pre-Columbian Cultures of the Lesser Antilles,* pp. 232–238. N.p.

Guarch Delmonte, José M.

1973 *Ensayo de Reconstrucción Etno-histórica del Taíno de Cuba. Série Arqueológica 4.* Instituto de Arqueología, Academia de Ciencias de Cuba, La Habana.

Haag, William G.

1965 Pottery Typology in Certain Lesser Antilles. *American Antiquity* 1(2):242–245.

Haas, Mary R.

1954 Letter from Mary Haas to Julian Granberry concerning the Methods for the Reconstitution of Phonological and Morphological Systems for No-Longer Spoken Languages from Written Materials. Berkeley, California.

Hadel, Richard E.

1975 *A Dictionary of Central American Carib.* 3 Vols. Belize Institute of Social Research and Action, Belize.

Hahn, Paul G.

1960 The Cayo Redondo Culture and Its Chronology. Ph.D. Dissertation, Department of Anthropology, Yale University, New Haven.

Harrington, M. R.

1921 *Cuba before Columbus.* 2 Vols. *Indian Notes and Monographs* 17, pts. 1–2. National Museum of the American Indian, Heye Foundation, New York.

Haviser, Jay B.

1997 Settlement Strategies in the Early Ceramic Age. In *The Indigenous People of the Caribbean,* edited by Samuel M. Wilson, pp. 57–69. University Press of Florida, Gainesville.

1998 First Contact from the Discoverer's View: The Native American Role 500 Years Ago. In *Now, Curaçao.* Jonckheer and Hagens, Curaçao.

Hernández Aquino, Luis

1977   *Diccionario de Voces Indígenas de Puerto Rico.* Editorial Cultural, Río Piedras.

1993   *Diccionario de Voces Indígenas de Puerto Rico.* 3rd ed. Editorial Cultural, Río Piedras.

Highfield, Arnold R.

1993   Toward a Language History of the Danish West Indies and the U.S. Virgin Islands. Vol. 1: *The Danish Presence and Legacy in the Virgin Islands,* edited by Svend E. Holsoe and John H. McCollum, pp. 123–139. St. Croix Landmarks Society, Frederiksted.

1997   Some Observations on the Taino Language. In *The Indigenous People of the Caribbean,* edited by Samuel M. Wilson, pp. 154–168. University Press of Florida, Gainesville.

Hoffman, Charles A., Jr.

1970   The Palmetto Grove Site on San Salvador, Bahamas. *Contributions to the Florida State Museum, Social Sciences* 16:1–16. Florida State Museum, Gainesville.

1974   Multilinear Evolution in the Prehistoric West Indies. In *Proceedings of the Fifth International Congress for the Study of the Pre-Columbian Cultures of the Lesser Antilles, Antigua, July 22–28, 1973,* pp. 143–152. Antigua National Trust and the Antigua Archaeological Society, Antigua.

1980   The Outpost Concept and the Mesoamerican Connection. In *Proceedings of the Eighth International Congress for the Study of the Pre-Columbian Cultures of the Lesser Antilles,* edited by Suzanne M. Lewenstein, pp. 307–316. *Anthropological Research Papers No. 22,* Arizona State University, Tempe.

Hofman, Corinne L.

1995   Three Late Prehistoric Sites in the Periphery of Guadeloupe: Grand Anse, Terre de Bas, and Morne Cybèle 1 and 2, la Désirade. Paper presented at the Sixteenth International Congress for Caribbean Archaeology, Basse-Terre, Guadeloupe.

Hofman, Corinne L., and Menno L. P. Hoogland

1991   Ceramic Developments on Saba, N.A. (350–1450 A.D.). In *Proceedings of the Fourteenth Congress of the International Association for Caribbean Archaeology.* Barbados Museum and Historical Society, Barbados.

Holt, Dennis

1999   *Tol (Jicaque). Languages of the World/Materials* 170. Lincom Europa, Munich.

Howard, R. A., and E. S. Howard, editors

1983   *Alexander Anderson's Geography and History of St. Vincent, West Indies.* President and Fellows of Harvard College and the Linnean Society of London, Cambridge, Mass.

Howells, W. W.

1966   Population Distances: Biological, Linguistic, Geographical, and Environmental. *Current Anthropology* 7:531–540.

Hulme, Peter

1986   *Colonial Encounters: Europe and the Native Caribbean, 1492–1797.* Methuen, New York.

Hulme, Peter, and Neil L. Whitehead

1992   *Wild Majesty: Encounters with Caribs from Columbus to the Present Day.* Clarendon Press, Oxford.

Joseph, Garnette

    1997   Five Hundred Years of Indigenous Resistance. In *The Indigenous People of the Caribbean,* edited by Samuel M. Wilson, pp. 214–222. University Press of Florida, Gainesville.

Kauffman, Terrence S., and William M. Norman

    1984   An Outline of Proto-Cholan Phonology, Morphology, and Vocabulary. In *Phoneticism in Mayan Hieroglyphic Writing,* edited by John S. Justeson and Lyle Campbell, pp.77–166. Institute for Mesoamerican Studies, State University of New York at Albany, *Publication No. 9.* Institute for Mesoamerican Studies, Albany.

Keegan, William F.

    1985   *Dynamic Horticulturalists: Population Expansion in the Prehistoric Bahamas.* University Microfilms International, Ann Arbor.

    1989   Creating the Guanahatabey (Ciboney): The Modern Genesis of an Extinct Culture. *Antiquity* 63:373–379.

    1997   *Bahamian Archaeology: Life in The Bahamas and Turks and Caicos before Columbus.* Media Publishing, Nassau.

Keegan, William F., and Betsy Carlson

    1997   *The Coralie Site, Grand Turk.* In *Times of the Islands: The International Magazine of the Turks and Caicos,* Summer Issue. Providenciales, Turks and Caicos Islands.

Keegan, William F., and Morgan D. Maclachlan

    1989   The Evolution of Avunculocal Chiefdoms: A Reconstruction of Taino Kinship and Politics. *American Anthropologist* 91(3):613–630.

Kerns, Virginia

    1983   *Women and the Ancestors: Black Carib Kinship and Ritual.* University of Illinois Press, Urbana.

Kozłowski, Janusz K.

    1975   Preceramic Cultures in the Caribbean. *Zeszyty Naukowe Uniwersytetu Jagiellońskiego,* No. 366, Prace Archeologiczne, No. 20. Uniwersytetu Jagiellońskiego, Kraków.

    1980   In Search of the Evolutionary Pattern of the Preceramic Cultures of the Caribbean. Museo del Hombre Dominicano. *Boletín* 13:61–79.

Krieger, Herbert W.

    1929   *Archaeological and Historical Investigations in Samaná, Dominican Republic.* United States National Museum, *Bulletin* 147. United States National Museum, Washington, D.C.

    1937   The Bahama Islands and their Prehistoric Population. *Smithsonian Institution Explorations and Field Work,* 1936:93–98.

Labat, R. P. J. B.

    1979   *Nouveau Voyage aux Isles de l'Amérique.* 5 vols. Courtinard, Saint-Joseph, France.

Lafleur, G.

    1992   *Les Caraïbes des Petites Antilles.* Karthala, Paris.

Langdon, Margaret

    1979   Some Thoughts on Hokan. In *The Languages of Native America,* edited by Lyle Campbell and Marianne Mithun, pp. 592–649. University of Texas Press, Austin.

Las Casas, Bartolomé de

1875   *Historia de las Indias.* [1527–1563] 5 Vols. As *Colección de Documentos Inéditos para la Historia de España,* Vols. 62–66. Madrid.

1909   *Apologética Historia de las Indias.* [1545?] Vol. 1 of *Historiadores de Indias,* edited by Daniel Serrano y Sanz. Bailly, Baillière e Hijos, Madrid.

1951   *Brevísima Relación de La destruccion de las Indias.* Prólogo y Selección de Agustín Millares Carlo, Mexico City.

Loukotka, Cestmír

1968   *Classification of South American Indian Languages.* Edited by Johannes Wilber. *Reference Series,* vol. 7. University of California at Los Angeles Latin American Center, Los Angeles.

Lovén, Sven

1935   *Origins of the Tainan Culture, West Indies.* Erlanders Boktryckeri Aktiebolag, Göteborg.

Lundberg, Emily R.

1989   Preceramic Procurement Patterns at Krum Bay, Virgin Islands. Unpublished Ph.D. Dissertation, Department of Anthropology, University of Illinois, Urbana.

1991   Interrelationships among Preceramic Complexes of Puerto Rico and the Virgin Islands. In *Proceedings of the Thirteenth International Congress for Caribbean Archaeology, Held in Willemstad, Curaçao, on July 24–29, 1989,* pp. 73–85. Archaeological-Anthropological Institute of the Netherlands Antilles, Willemstad.

MacLaury, James C.

1970   Archaeological Investigations on Cat Island, Bahamas. *Contributions of the Florida State Museum, Social Sciences* 16:27–50. Florida State Museum, Gainesville.

MacNeish, Richard S.

1982   *Final Annual Report of the Belize Archaic Archaeological Reconnaissance.* Center for Archaeological Studies, Boston University, Boston.

Major, R. H.

1870   *Select Letters of Christopher Columbus with other Original Documents.* Translated and edited by R. H. Major. Hakluyt Society No. 43, London.

Marvel, Josiah

1988   *Lucaiarum Tabula Onomastica: A Toponymy of the Lucayan Archipelago.* Preliminary draft. Providenciales, Turks and Caicos Islands.

Mason, John Alden

1950   The Languages of South American Indians. In *Bureau of American Ethnology Bulletin 143, Handbook of South American Indians,* edited by Julian H. Steward, pp. 157–317. Smithsonian Institution, Washington, D.C.

Matteson, Esther

1972   Proto-Arawakan. In *Comparative Studies in Amerindian Languages,* by Esther Matteson, Alva Wheeler, Frances L. Jackson, Nathan E. Waltz, and Diana R. Christian, pp. 160–242. *Janua Linguarum, Series Practica* 127. Mouton, The Hague.

McAlister, Lyle

1984   *Spain and Portugal in the New World, 1492–1700.* University of Minnesota Press, Minneapolis.

McKusick, Marshall

1960   Distribution of Ceramic Styles in the Lesser Antilles, West Indies. Unpublished Ph.D. Dissertation, Department of Anthropology, Yale University, New Haven.

1970   Aboriginal Canoes in the West Indies. In *Papers in Caribbean Anthropology,* compiled by Sidney W. Mintz. *Yale University Publications in Anthropology, No. 63.* Yale University Press, New Haven.

McQuown, Norman

1955   The Indigenous Languages of Latin America. *American Anthropologist* 57:501–570.

Meggers, Betty J., and Clifford Evans

1980   Un Método Cerámico para el Reconocimiento de Comunidades Pre-Históricas. Museo del Hombre Dominicano, *Boletín* 14:57–73.

Migliazza, Ernest C.

1985   Languages of the Orinoco-Amazon Region: Current Status. In *South American Indian Languages: Retrospect and Prospect,* edited by Harriet E. Manelis Klein and Louisa R. Stark, pp. 17–139. University of Texas Press, Austin.

Moore, Clark

1982   Investigation of Preceramic Sites on Île-à-Vache, Haiti. *The Florida Anthropologist* 35(4):186–199.

Morse, Birgit Faber

1997   The Salt River Site, St. Croix, at the Time of the Encounter. In *The Indigenous People of the Caribbean,* edited by Samuel M. Wilson, pp. 36–45. University Press of Florida, Gainesville.

Morales Patiño, Oswaldo

1947   Cayo Ocampo: Historia de un Cayo. *Revista de Arqueología y Etnología,* Serie 2, Año I, Época II, No. 4-5:55–123. Habana.

Moreau, Jean-Pierre

1988   *Guide des Trésors Archéologiques Sous-Marins des Petites Antilles: D'Après les Archives Anglaises, Espagnoles, et Françaises des XVI, XVII, et XVIII Siècles.* J.-P. Moreau, Clamart, France.

1991   Les Caraïbes Insulaires et la Mer Aux Seizième et Dix-septième Siècles d'Après les Sources Ethnohistoriques. *Journal de la Société des Américanistes* 77:63–75.

1992   *Les Petites Antilles de Christophe Colomb à Richelieu (1493–1635).* Karthala, Paris.

Morse, Birgit Faber

1997   The Salt River Site, St. Croix, at the Time of the Encounter. In *The Indigenous People of the Caribbean,* edited by Samuel M. Wilson, pp. 36–45. University Press of Florida, Gainesville.

Noble, J. Kingsley

1965   *Proto-Arawak and Its Descendants.* Indiana University Press, Bloomington.

Ober, Frederick

1877   Wordlists of Dominican and Vincentian (Island) Carib. National Anthropological Archives, Ms. 1084.

1879   Ornithological Exploration of the Caribee Islands. *Annual Report of the Smithsonian Institution,* pp. 446–451.

Oliver, José R.

1989   The Archaeological, Linguistic, and Ethnohistorical Evidence for the Expansion of Arawakan into Northwestern Venezuela and Northeastern Colombia. Unpublished Ph.D. Dissertation, Department of Anthropology, University of Illinois, Urbana.

1992a   The Caguana Ceremonial Center in Puerto Rico: A Cosmic Journey through Taino Spatial and Iconographic Symbolism. Paper presented at the Tenth International Symposium of Latin American Indian Literatures, San Juan.

1992b   Chican-Taíno Iconography and Spatial Symbolism. Paper presented at the Ninety-first Annual Meeting of the American Anthropological Association, San Francisco.

1993   El Centro Ceremonial de Caguana. Un Análisis Interpretativo del Simbolismo Iconográfico y de la Cosmovisión Taína de Borinquén. Unpublished manuscript.

1997   The Taino Cosmos. In *The Indigenous People of the Caribbean,* edited by Samuel M. Wilson, pp. 140–153. University Press of Florida, Gainesville.

Ortega, Elpídio, and José Guerrero

1982   El Fechado del Sitio Meillcoide Bois de Charrité, Haiti. Museo del Hombre Dominicano, *Boletín* 17:29–53.

Osgood, Cornelius

1942   *The Ciboney Culture of Cayo Redondo, Cuba. Yale University Publications in Anthropology 25.* Yale University Press, New Haven.

Oviedo y Valdez, Gonzalo Fernández de

1851   *Historia General y Natural de las Indias, Islas e Tierra Firme del Mar Océano.* [1547] 4 Vols. Madrid.

Pantel, A. Gus

1988   Precolumbian Flaked Stone Assemblages in the West Indies. Unpublished Ph.D. Dissertation, Department of Anthropology, University of Tennessee, Knoxville.

Payne, David L.

1990   Some Widespread Grammatical Forms in South American Languages. In *Amazonian Linguistics: Studies in Lowland South American Languages,* edited by Doris L. Payne., pp. 75–87. University of Texas Press, Austin.

Pelleprat, Pierre

1665   *Introduction a la Langue des Galibis.* S. & G. Cramoisy, Paris.

Petitjean-Roget, Henry

1997a   The Taino Vision: A Study in the Exchange of Misunderstanding. In *The Indigenous Peoples of the Caribbean,* edited by Samuel M. Wilson, pp. 169–175. University of Alabama Press, Tuscaloosa.

1997b   Notes on Ancient Caribbean Art and Mythology. In *The Indigenous People of the Caribbean,* edited by Samuel M. Wilson, pp. 100–108. University Press of Florida, Gainesville.

Rainey, Froelich G.

1940   *Porto Rican Archaeology. Scientific Survey of Porto Rico and the Virgin Islands,* vol. 18(1). New York Academy of Sciences, New York.

1952   *Porto Rican Prehistory. Scientific Survey of Porto Rico and the Virgin Islands,* vol. 18(1). New York Academy of Sciences, New York.

Rainey, Froelich, and Juan Ortiz Aguilú

1983   Bois Neuf: The Archeological View from West-Central Haiti. *Proceedings of the Tenth International Congress for the Study of Pre-Columbian Cultures of the Lesser Antilles.* Fort-de-France, Martinique.

Rat, J. N.

1898   The Caribe Language as Now Spoken in Dominica, West Indies. *Journal of the Anthropological Institute of Great Britain and Ireland* 27:293–315.

Rodríguez, Miguel

1991   Arqueología de Punto Candelero, Puerto Rico. In *Proceedings of the Thirteenth International Congress for Caribbean Archaeology, Held in Willemstad, Curaçao, on July 24–29, 1989,* pp. 605–627. Archaeological-Anthropological Institute of the Netherlands Antilles, Willemstad.

1997   Religious Beliefs of the Saladoid People. In *The Indigenous People of the Caribbean,* edited by Samuel M. Wilson, pp. 80–87. University Press of Florida, Gainesville.

Roosevelt, Anna C.

1980   *Parmaná: Prehistoric Maize and Manioc Subsistence along the Amazon and Orinoco.* Academic Press, New York.

Rouse, Irving

1942   *Archeology of the Maniabón Hills, Cuba. Yale University Publications in Anthropology 26.* Yale University Press, New Haven.

1947   Ciboney Artifacts from Île-à-Vache, Haiti. *Bulletin du Bureau d'Ethnologie de la République d'haiti,* Série II, No. 2:16–21, No. 3:62–66. Port-Au-Prince.

1951   Areas and Periods of Culture in the Greater Antilles. *Southwestern Journal of Anthropology* 7:248–265.

1952   *Porto Rican Prehistory. Scientific Survey of Porto Rico and the Virgin Islands* vol. 18 (3–4). New York Academy of Sciences, New York.

1982   The Olsen Collection from Île-à-Vache, Haiti. *The Florida Anthropologist* 35(4): 168–185.

1986   *Migrations in Prehistory: Inferring Population Movements from Cultural Remains.* Yale University Press, New Haven.

1987   Origin and Development of the Indians Discovered by Columbus. In *Columbus and His World: Proceedings of the First San Salvador Conference,* pp. 293–312. College Center of the Finger Lakes, Bahamian Field Station, San Salvador, Bahamas.

1992   *The Tainos: Rise and Decline of the People Who Greeted Columbus.* Yale University Press, New Haven.

Rouse, Irving, and Louis Allaire

1979   Cronología del Caribe. Museo del Hombre Dominicano, *Boletín* 12:59–117.

Rouse, Irving, and José M. Cruxent

1963   *Venezuelan Archaeology.* Yale University Press, New Haven.

Salzano, F. M., J. V. Neel, H. Gershowitz, and E. C. Migliazza

1977   Intra and Intertribal Genetic Variation within a Linguistic Group: The Gê-Speaking Indians of Brazil. *American Journal of Physical Anthropology* 47:337–348.

Sears, William H., and Shaun D. Sullivan
    1978   Bahamas Prehistory. *American Antiquity* 43(1):3–25.
Spielman, Richard S., Ernest C. Migliazza, and James V. Neel
    1977   Regional Linguistics and Genetic Differences among Yanomama Indians. *Science* 184:637–644.
Stevens-Arroyo, Antonio M.
    1988   *Cave of the Jagua: The Mythological World of the Tainos.* University of New Mexico Press, Albuquerque.
Stokes, Anne V., and William F. Keegan
    1998   *A Settlement Survey for Prehistoric Archaeological Sites on Grand Cayman. Miscellaneous Project Report No. 52,* Florida Museum of Natural History, Gainesville.
Sued Badillo, Jalil
    1978   *Los Caribes, Realidad o Fábula: Ensayos de Rectificación Histórica.* Editorial Antillana, Río Piedras.
Sullivan, Shaun D.
    1980   An Overview of the 1976 to 1978 Archeological Investigations in the Caicos Islands. *The Florida Anthropologist* 33(3):120–142.
    1981   Prehistoric Patterns of Exploitation and Colonization in the Turks and Caicos Islands. Unpublished Ph.D. Dissertation, Department of Anthropology, University of Illinois, Urbana.
Tabío, Ernesto E., and Estrella Rey
    1979   *Prehistoria de Cuba.* Editorial de Ciencias Sociales, La Habana.
Taylor, Douglas M.
    1951a   Morphophonemics of Island-Carib (Central American Dialect). *International Journal of American Linguistics* 17:224–234.
    1951b   *The Black Carib of British Honduras. Viking Fund Publications in Archaeology* 17. Wenner-Gren Foundation, New York.
    1952   The Principal Grammatical Formatives of Island Carib (C. A. Dialect). *International Journal of American Linguistics* 18(3):150–165.
    1953   A Note on the Identification of Some Island-Carib Suffixes. *International Journal of American Linguistics* 19:195–200.
    1954   Diachronic Note on the Carib Contribution to Island-Carib. *International Journal of American Linguistics* 20:28–33.
    1955   Phonemes of the Hopkins (British Honduras) Dialect of Island-Carib (Island-Carib I). *International Journal of American Linguistics* 21:233–241.
    1956a   Languages and Ghost-Languages of the West Indies. *International Journal of American Linguistics* 22:180–183.
    1956b   Island-Carib II: Word Classes, Affixes, Verbs, Nouns. *International Journal of American Linguistics* 22:1–44
    1956c   Island-Carib III: Locators, Particles. *International Journal of American Linguistics* 22:138–150.
    1958a   Island-Carib IV: Syntactic Notes, Texts. *International Journal of American Linguistics* 24:36–60.
    1958b   The Place of Island-Carib within the Arawakan Family. *International Journal of American Linguistics* 24:153–156.

1969   A Preliminary View of Arawak Phonology. *International Journal of American Linguistics* 35:234–238.

1977   *Languages of the West Indies.* The Johns Hopkins University Press, Baltimore.

Taylor, Douglas M., and Berend J. Hoff

1980   The Linguistic Repertory of the Island-Carib in the Seventeenth Century: The Men's Language (A Carib Pidgin?). *International Journal of American Linguistics* 46(4):301–312.

Taylor, Douglas M., and Irving Rouse

1955   Linguistic and Archaeological Time-depth in the West Indies. *International Journal of American Linguistics* 21:105–115.

Tejera, Emiliano

1951   *Palabras Indíjenas de la Isla de Santo Domingo, con Adiciones por Emilio Tejera.* Ciudad Trujillo: Editores del Caribe.

Tejera, Emilio

1977   *Indigenismos.* 2 vols. Editora de Santo Domingo, Santo Domingo.

Thomas, Léon

1953   La Dominique et les Derniers Caraïbes Insulaires. *Cahiers d'Outre-Mer* 6:37–60.

Turner, E. Daymond, Jr.

1985   Forgotten Treasure from The Indies: The Illustrations and Drawings of Fernández de Oviedo. *Huntington Library Quarterly* 48:1–46.

Vega, Bernardo

1980   *Los Cacicazgos de la Hispaniola.* Ediciones del Museo del Hombre Dominicano, Santo Domingo.

Vegamián, F.

1951   ¿Cómo es la Guajira? *Tercera Conferencia Interamericana de Agricultura,* pp. 11–33. Caracas.

Veloz Maggiolo, Marcio

1976   *Medioambiente y Adaptación Humana en la Prehistoria de Santo Domingo,* Vol. 1. Editorial de la Universidad Autónoma de Santo Domingo, Santo Domingo.

1980   *Las Sociedades Arcáicas de Santo Domingo.* Museo del Hombre Dominicano, Serie Investigaciones Antropológicas, No. 16; Fundación García Arévalo, Serie Investigaciones, No. 12. Santo Domingo.

Veloz Maggiolo, Marcio, and Elpidio Ortega

1973   *El Precerámico de Santo Domingo: Nuevos Lugares y Posible Relación con otros Puntos del Area Antillana.* Museo del Hombre Dominicano, *Papeles Ocasionales* No. 1. Museo del Hombre Dominicano, Santo Domingo.

1976   The Preceramic of the Dominican Republic: Some New Finds and Their Possible Relationships. In *Proceedings of the First Puerto Rican Symposium on Archaeology,* edited by Linda S. Robinson, pp. 142–201. Fundación Arqueológica, Antropológica e Histórica de Puerto Rico, San Juan.

Veloz Maggiolo, Marcio, Elpidio Ortega, and Ángel Caba Fuentes

1981   *Los Modos de Vida Meillacoides y Sus Posibles Orígenes.* Museo del Hombre Dominicano, Santo Domingo.

Vescelius, Gary S.

Ms   Notes on Tainan Languages, N.D. In the possession of Julian Granberry, Horse-
       shoe Beach, Florida.

Vivanco, Julián

1946   *El Lenguaje de los Indios de Cuba*. Editorial Ilustración Panamericana.

Watters, David R.

1980   Transect Surveying and Prehistoric Site Locations on Barbuda and Montserrat,
         Leeward Islands, West Indies. Ph.D. dissertation, Department of Anthropology,
         University of Pittsburgh, Pittsburgh.

1997   Maritime Trade in the Prehistoric Eastern Caribbean. In *The Indigenous People
         of the Caribbean*, edited by Samuel M. Wilson, pp. 88–99. University Press of
         Florida, Gainesville.

2001   Historical Archaeology in the British Caribbean. In *Island Lives: Historical Ar-
         chaeologies of the Caribbean*, edited by Paul Farnsworth, pp. 81–88. The Univer-
         sity of Alabama Press, Tuscaloosa.

Watts, D.

1987   *The West Indies: Patterns of Development, Culture and Environmental Change
         Since 1492*. Cambridge University Press, Cambridge.

Wilbert, Johannes

1957   Prólogo. In *Diccionario Guarao-Español, Español-Guarao*, by Basilio María de
         Barral. Sociedad de Ciencias Naturales La Salle, *Monografías* 3:7–18. Ediciones
         Sucre, Caracas.

1972   *Survivors of Eldorado*. Praeger, New York.

Williams, James

1928   The Warau Indians of Guiana and Vocabulary of Their Language. *Journal de la
         Société des Américanistes de Paris*, New Series 20:193–252.

1929   The Warau Language of Guiana and Vocabulary of Their Language. *Journal de
         la Société des Américanistes de Paris*, New Series 21:201–261.

Wilson, Samuel M.

1990   *Hispaniola: Caribbean Chiefdoms in the Age of Columbus*. The University of Ala-
         bama Press, Tuscaloosa.

1997   *The Indigenous People of the Caribbean*, edited by Samuel M. Wilson. University
         Press of Florida, Gainesville.

Winter, John

1987   Current Research. *American Antiquity* 52(1):192–193.

Winter, John, and Mark Gilstrap

1991   Preliminary Results of Ceramic Analysis and the Movements of Populations
         into The Bahamas. *Proceedings of the Twelfth International Congress for Carib-
         bean Archaeology, 1987*, pp. 371–386. Cayenne.

Wise, Mary Ruth

1990   Valence-Changing Affixes in Maipuran Arawakan Languages. In *Amazonian
         Linguistics: Studies in Lowland South American Languages*, edited by Doris L.
         Payne, pp. 89–116. University of Texas Press, Austin.

Yacou, A.

1992   *Christophe Colomb et la Découverte de la Guadeloupe.* Editions Caribéennes, Paris.

Yacou, A., and J. Adelaide-Merlande, editors

1993   *La Découverte et la Conquête de la Guadeloupe.* CERC, Point-à-Pitre, Guadeloupe, and Karthala, Paris.

Zayas Y Alfonso, Alfredo

1931   *Lexicografía Antillana: Diccionario de Voces usadas por los aborígenes de las Antillas Mayores y de algunas de las Menores y consideraciones acerca de su Significado y de su Formación.* 2d edition. In 2 Vols. Tipos. Molina y Cía, Habana.

Index